PRAISE FOR *THE OLD WAYS*

"A volume to refer to at every Moon, at each turning of the wheel, and whenever the Otherworld needs to be consulted."

—**ELLEN EVERT HOPMAN,** author of *The Real Witches of New England*

"A truly invaluable resource for anyone interested in Hedge Witchcraft. The author adeptly weaves together information from the past while also helping the reader with skills and exercises that they can use in the present in order to continue their path."

—**ROBIN CORAK,** author of *Dream Magick* and *Persephone*

"An absolute treasure. Joanna dives well below the surface to bring us fresh explorations of core aspects of a witch's practice: working with different types of energy, the ethics of magic, the importance of self-discovery and self-awareness, and how we integrate our practice into daily life....Best of all, she generously shares her personal experiences with the topics discussed in each chapter, in lyrical prose that places the reader right there with her in her beloved landscapes. The book is rich with practical suggestions, exercises, spells and herbal recipes, beautiful sabbat rituals, and invigorating lunar rituals."

—**LISA CHAMBERLAIN,** author of *Herbs of the Year Spellbook* and
    Self-Care for Witches

"If you loved Joanna's book *The Path of the Hedge Witch*, I guarantee you are going to find new depths of appreciation for *The Old Ways*. It is full of wonderful ways to dive deeper into your craft, be it a solo path or a group path. There is something for everyone in this book!"

—**ERON MAZZA,** podcast host and author

"An important contribution to the growing field of witchcraft and Paganism....In a beautiful interweaving of explanation, exercise, and example, the injections of Joanna's own personal experiences help to anchor and clarify the book's material....A powerful invitation to access the wisdom of the whole self and deepen one's connection to nature."

—**TIFFANY LAZIC,** author of *The Great Work*

"Throughout the whole book, the three foundations of Hedge Witchcraft are woven—a willingness to walk between worlds, ability to work alone and a love of nature, enabling anyone, from novice to experienced practitioner to gain new understanding. Joanna uses her own examples as an illustration to each of these topics with beautiful clarity....This is a fantastic instructional guide to taking your Hedge Witchcraft further into a profound and more nuanced level. It is a spellbinding read!"

—**THEA PROTHERO,** author of *A Guide to Pilgrimage*

"This is a concise and straightforward guide to what a Hedge Witch is and how to be one. For those who are not sure of their path, this has many commonalities with Traditional Witchcraft, Wicca, and Neo-Druidry, but it is a distinct path of itself, laid out with clarity here....This book will teach you and help you to create your own practices over time."

—**LUKE EASTWOOD,** author of *The Druid Garden* and *A Path Through the Forest*

"A rich and enjoyable read filled with wisdom grounded in useful tools and practices for weaving into everyday life. Joanna van der Hoeven explains clearly what a magical life is all about, always encouraging the reader to widen their perspective and deepen their connection with the Otherworld and themselves."

—**SHEENA CUNDY,** author of *The Witch Wavelength* and *Riches for Witches*

THE OLD
WAYS

About the Author

Joanna van der Hoeven has been working in Pagan traditions for nearly thirty years. She is an author, teacher, dancer, blogger, photographer, and videographer. Her love of nature and the land where she lives provide her with constant inspiration. She was born in Quebec, Canada, and now lives near the sea in Suffolk, England.

THE OLD
WAYS

A Hedge Witch's
Guide to Living a
Magical Life

JOANNA VAN DER HOEVEN

foreword by Rae Beth

LLEWELLYN
WOODBURY, MINNESOTA

FIRST EDITION
First Printing, 2025

Book design by Rebecca Zins
Cover art by Selcha Uni
Cover design by Shira Atakpu

Llewellyn Publications is a registered trademark of Llewellyn Worldwide Ltd.

Library of Congress Cataloging-In-Publication Data
Names: Hoeven, Joanna van der, author. | Beth, Rae, writer of foreword.
Title: The old ways : a hedge witch's guide to living a magical life /
    Joanna van der Hoeven ; foreword by Rae Beth.
Description: First edition. | Woodbury, MN : Llewellyn Publications, [2024]
    | Includes bibliographical references. | Summary: "The Old Ways deepens
    your skills in herbalism, spellcraft, hedge riding (trance work), and
    more so you can truly live your Craft. Following Joanna's guidance, you
    will develop a daily practice that involves connection to deity, the
    Fair Folk, and your familiar. Explore a thirteen-month lunar ritual
    series and create your own divination set based on your local
    surroundings. With this book you can expand your solitary practice and
    find your place in the world"—Provided by publisher.
Identifiers: LCCN 2024047368 (print) | LCCN 2024047369 (ebook) | ISBN
    9780738775517 (paperback) | ISBN 9780738775685 (ebook)
Subjects: LCSH: Witchcraft. | Magic. | Nature—Religious aspects.
Classification: LCC BF1571 .H629 2024 (print) | LCC BF1571 (ebook) | DDC
    203/.3—dc23/eng/20241231
LC record available at https://lccn.loc.gov/2024047368
LC ebook record available at https://lccn.loc.gov/2024047369

Llewellyn Worldwide Ltd. does not participate in, endorse, or have any authority or responsibility concerning private business transactions between our authors and the public.
    All mail addressed to the author is forwarded but the publisher cannot, unless specifically instructed by the author, give out an address or phone number.
    Any internet references contained in this work are current at publication time, but the publisher cannot guarantee that a specific location will continue to be maintained. Please refer to the publisher's website for links to authors' websites and other sources.

Llewellyn Publications
A Division of Llewellyn Worldwide Ltd.
2143 Wooddale Drive
Woodbury, MN 55125-2989
www.llewellyn.com
Printed in the United States of America

Contents

Part 3 Wisdom
Going Deeper

Part 4 Integration
Crafting Your Own Tradition

Foreword

When I wrote the first of my own Hedge Witch series, published back in 1990 by Robert Hale, I had no idea what was being started (or restarted). I now believe there are tutelary spirits of Hedge Witchcraft and that they want this tradition to be widely known and practiced. (I certainly don't believe I was the best person for the task of starting off an increased awareness of the idea of Hedge Witchcraft in our own times, only that I was at least available and willing!) Since then, there has been groundbreaking work by many writers, some simple and inspirational, some scholarly, and many adding something important to our collective knowledge. And now here are Joanna van der Hoeven's very fine books. The first one, *The Path of the Hedge Witch*, is an inspiration from start to finish. And the second, which you hold in your hands, contains a treasury of ideas and techniques for the lifestyle and practices of a hedge witch.

As the author explains, the term *hedge witch* comes partly from the nineteenth-century idea of a hedge priest or hedge school. A hedge priest was a wandering preacher not attached to any church or organisation but autonomous and self-motivated. A hedge school was an informal thing such as a group of people learning to read and write with no official backing or assistance. The hedge witch is similarly free—a free spirit. This independent stance is honoured one hundred percent by Joanna van der Hoeven as her work is entirely free from dogma, concerned only to assist her readers in their own magical creativity and explorations. As she makes clear, there cannot be a last word on Hedge Witchcraft because a hedge witch is always learning, and also because our practices change in response to changing times and adapt endlessly to new inspirations and the particular skills of each hedge witch.

There are other terms underlying the tradition of Hedge Witchcraft, and these are older and more specific. The first is the *haegtessa*, the hedge rider, and there is also the *haegzissa*, the hedge sitter, from Germanic tradition. The ideas conveyed by these terms underpin our modern practice. But it would be a mistake to think that all Hedge Witchcraft was and is solely Germanic, for aspects of it are found in other cultures as well. And today, we can feel entirely free to interpret the basic themes of Hedge Witchcraft in alignment with our own culture and environment, wherever in the world we happen to live. For we cannot know with any certainty how they were perceived or enacted in the past.

What are these basic themes? What exactly does a hedge witch do? Specifically, she flies beyond the hedge that symbolically surrounds the living human community or settlement in which she dwells. In other words, she takes a spirit journey to speak with, see, sense, or in whatever way commune with various spirits, including ancestors, elementals, elves, nature spirits, and deities. This is not only to gain allies and assistance in magical work; it is also for the increase of understanding, healing, and peace between this everyday world and the otherworld of nature's soul. Traditionally, so far as we know, a hedge witch also would have been expected to do such things as protect her community from any form of psychic attack as well as calm the earthbound dead and gain assistance for them in coming to terms with death and moving on.

The methods advocated here by Joanna van der Hoeven are for the most part a preparation for such work rather than the work itself. You can't be strong magically unless you have some measure of what she mentions in her book—knowledge, wisdom, and experience. The methods seem invariably gentle and easy-going, but don't be fooled! They are based in discipline and commitment and respect for those of the otherworld as well as for the many, many species and spirits of our own world. As she continually points out, when working with spirits, we are expected to give (in accordance with our own abilities, resources, and ethics) as well as receive. However, the offerings required of us can be surprisingly simple, especially in comparison to what we are asking, and still be acceptable.

In other words, for our spirit work to be effective and life-enhancing, we need to be firmly rooted in a balanced approach. For this, being a hedge witch requires us to learn certain magical skills, to make and do things as necessary, but most of all it requires us to craft or shape ourselves and our self-understanding. And this really is the book's bottom line. So we need to become fully aware that we are a part of nature, not apart from it, and that our spells and spirit journeys are interconnected with all that is. A genuine hedge witch knows this in her bones and blood and not merely as a concept. This is the theme of *The Old Ways*. Within it, the author brings us many ideas, practices, rites, and spells concerning how we might craft ourselves successfully. Some are drawn from the wider community; some are simple common sense; and most are specific to magical practitioners. This wise and subtle book is grounded firmly in nature's tides and cycles, and it speaks from the heart. Personally, I feel that the tutelary spirits of Hedge Witchcraft are delighted with it!

Rae Beth
WEST OF ENGLAND, 2024

Introduction

You never stop learning.

These are probably the four most important words for any hedge witch. When you are working in your practice or your craft, it is paramount you accept that you will never know everything there is to know about Hedge Witchcraft, or anything else for that matter, and that there is always more to learn, integrate, and investigate.

That is one of the true joys of this path.

That is also why I've written this second book on Hedge Witchcraft. My first book, *The Path of the Hedge Witch*, was a solid introduction that also could serve as a refresher for those who walk between the worlds. It is highly recommended that you first read *The Path of the Hedge Witch* to gain a solid foundation in this work.

In this second book, we now go deeper into the tradition of the hedge witch, exploring past practitioners of the craft, looking at folklore and how that might intertwine with your own environment. We also delve into more personal work in order for our hedge ridings to be better performed and more rewarding. We will integrate ourselves with the deities, the seasons, and the cycles of the moon as well as begin crafting an intimate relationship with the witch's familiar. We will also have an examined look at magic and ethics, detailed instruction on herbcrafting, and how to start your own divination practice. Finally, we put it all together and understand that being a hedge witch truly is about what you do, not just what you think or believe. It is walking the talk.

Is this an intermediate book? Well, that depends of how you define intermediate. Moving from being a beginner in the craft to one who has advanced in their practice can only be achieved through experience, which is something that simply cannot be taught. I can point out certain directions you may wish to take in your journey, but I cannot walk it for you. This book is a continuation on the journey—a new vista that opens up when you have reached your first destination, inspires you to search out new paths based upon your past knowledge and experience, and culminates in an innate wisdom of your own Hedge Witchcraft practice.

There are some exercises provided in this book to help deepen your practice. I strongly recommend that you do the exercises, for they will help you truly understand what it is that you are reading on a more visceral level, rather than simply an intellectual one. I also offer some further reading on certain subjects from authors that I have found resonance with and can heartily recommend. Don't just read this book; do the work too! I promise that you will come away with some new insight if only you do the work. As well, you will truly get your money's worth taking this book not only at face value but also as planned lessons that can help further your own craft.

There are so many different ways of being a hedge witch. This book is based upon my own learning and decades of experience in the tradition. It will indubitably vary from the practice of another hedge witch, for we each come into our craft through our own life experiences. Parts of this book may resonate deeply with you; others may not. Take what you desire from this book and further your own journey and experience, for being a hedge witch is a path that only you can walk. No one can walk it for you.

In *The Path of the Hedge Witch*, each chapter ended with a little story—a snapshot in time for a hedge witch who is walking her talk. This was written in the third person, but, as many of you have already guessed, it is autobiographical. I have done the same for this work, but I have now written it in the first person in order to cut through any bias and hopefully speak directly to your heart.

May you be blessed upon your journey in this world and the otherworld.

Joanna van der Hoeven

IMBOLC 2023

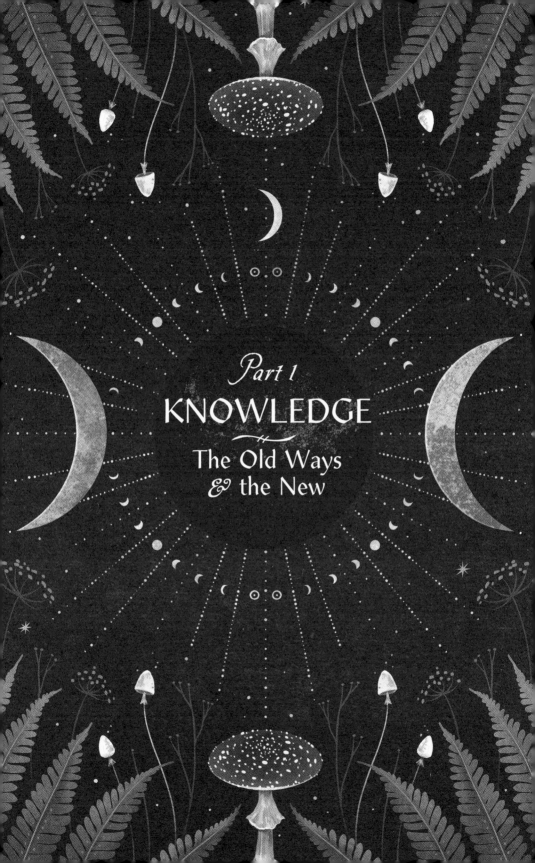

Part 1
KNOWLEDGE

The Old Ways
& the New

Chapter 1

The Cunning Folk

You don't have to be crazy to do
this, but it sure does help.

Bob Ross, *The Joy of Painting*

The past is an important teacher. It is essential to have an understanding of the past so that we can learn from it, both the good and the bad, in order to not repeat the mistakes that have been made by those who have gone before. It is also how we learn where we can go in the present moment with honour and integrity, for a better future for all. The craft of the hedge witch is formed from both the old ways and the new.

We begin our exploration of the craft of the hedge witch by looking at the cunning folk from our past history. The cunning folk were those who operated on the edges of society and yet worked for society. They were the healers, the midwives, the wisewomen and men of their communities. They knew where the herbs grew that could heal or harm; they knew the language of beasts and could foretell the future through observance of natural phenomena. They were the ones whose eyes and ears were open, who paid attention to the world around them, and who integrated themselves not only with the human world, but also with the other-than-human realms, often operating betwixt and between the worlds.

These were the folk who were *different*, who had come to terms with their separateness and who welcomed and worked with their own innate power. These were independent thinkers and doers with various agendas ranging from helping locals in a beneficial way to practising any kind of magic, both beneficial and malefic, to those who paid them. They knew their own minds and stood beyond the social norms of the day to practice their craft.

These were the practitioners of folk magic, as opposed to the ceremonial magicians often employed by the aristocracy before the beginnings of the Reformation, when all magical practices were subsequently deemed evil, Witchcraft and ceremonial magic alike. These cunning folk were the Toad-men and women, the Fairy Doctors, and the Pellars.[1] They worked alone, often performing their services alongside their usual occupations.[2] The cunning folk were solitary, as opposed to witches who reputedly mostly worked in covens, at least according to the confessions derived from torture during the infamous witch trials of the Middle Ages. It is this author's opinion that the covens alluded to in the Witchcraft trial confessions were little more than an attempt to bring more people into trial via the witch hunters, who made a lot of money on people they could accuse and charge for Witchcraft, and the possessions and property that were taken over from those accused, condemned, and killed for Witchcraft.

Today's hedge witch can be seen as a continuation of these cunning folk who worked on the edges of society. The hedge witch carries knowledge and wisdom of the natural world and is also a walker between the worlds. They are a solitary worker of the craft, with their own needs, desires, experience, and specialties. It is said that the cunning folk of the past would sometimes work to oppose the malefic magic of witches and Witchcraft.[3] However, today the words *witch* and *Witchcraft* are being reclaimed from their dark depths of bad publicity and historical inaccuracy and are mov-

---

1 *Pellar* may be a term that derives from "expeller," as in to expel spirits. Hutton, *The Triumph of the Moon*, 85.
2 Ibid., 98.
3 Davies, *Cunning-Folk*, 103.

ing into the light of day for what they truly are: a tradition of personal empowerment that allows an individual to access their talents, both inborn and learned, to become a functioning, contributing, and responsible member of their locality. At least, that's the theory; not all witches can or want to live up to that ideal. However, most of the ones that I know certainly do. Hence, most people today would associate Witchcraft with the cunning folk and their practices.

In this section we will look at several different cunning folk throughout history, their practices, and their importance to their community and sometimes to history as a whole. Their stories range from the tragic witch hunts of medieval Britain to more modern-day workers. By examining the wide range of their stories, I hope to provide an overview of what it meant historically to be a worker of the craft in all its various forms and how we can take what we learn from these past practitioners into the future.

Agnes Sampson

The demonization of the cunning folk began in earnest after the publication of the *Malleus Maleficarum* (*The Hammer of the Witches*) by Heinrich Kramer. King James VI of Scotland seized upon this newer view of those who practiced a form of magic as evil and out to get him specifically, and he ran with it, beginning the widespread witch hunts throughout Britain. Before then, malefic witches would be tried locally by their home constituency, but now outsiders from the church were brought in to decide the fate of those they deemed "witches." These new witch hunts began in Britain with the arrest of a woman named Agnes Sampson of Nether Keith, Scotland.[4]

King James VI wanted to show that he was a good king and felt he needed an enemy in order to do so. With dire winters in 1589–1591, a ready-made excuse for malefic Witchcraft was created and a scapegoat needed to be found. They found their "witch," one Agnes Sampson, who was known as a *grace wyff* (grace wife), a midwife, and a healer, otherwise known as "the Wyse Woman of Keith."

4 "The Witch Hunts," BBC 2 (aired January 21, 2023).

For many years, folk healers existed and worked within the boundaries of Catholicism, calling upon the saints, Jesus, and Mary in many of their charms. This did not sit well with the new fanatical branch of Protestantism that was sweeping the nation, with James VI seeing the power that it could provide. In King James's reign, the wording of the Bible was changed from "thou shalt not suffer a poisoner to live" to "thou shalt not suffer a witch to live." Sanctioned by the monarchy, witch hunts had formally begun in parts of Britain. Those who held power or who were perceived to have power in their community and who were not sanctioned by the new Protestant church were deemed the enemy.

Agnes was known to be a healer for both the common folk and the nobility. She was summoned to stand before a gathering of church clergy on September 15, 1589, a full year before she was formally accused of Witchcraft. They had their eyes on her and were waiting to make their move. A woman with power and authority was not something to be tolerated.

A new Scottish Witchcraft Act was created that now made Witchcraft a capital offense. However, this new act did not actually describe what Witchcraft was; therefore, it was up to the individuals to determine for themselves. This led, obviously, to widespread abuse. So, what was Agnes Sampson accused of?

She was accused of healing people. Fifty-three accounts of healing or attempting to heal people.[5]

Yes, you read that right. This "horrible witch" healed people.

Agnes had learned her healing craft from her father. She was described as being "grave, matron-like, and settled in her answers."[6] It is said that in her prayers for healing, she conjured her healing magic in the name of Christ and God.[7] So not only was she a healer, but she was also a Christian.

She was charged with Witchcraft and brought before the court and King James himself in Edinburgh. *The Newes from Scotland* stated that

5 "The Witch Hunts," BBC 2 (aired January 21, 2023).
6 "Sketches of Superstitions," Random Scottish History, https://random scottishhistory.com/2020/12/31/sketches-of-superstitions-saturday -july-18-1840-pp-206-207 (accessed January 23, 2023).
7 "The Witch Hunts," BBC 2 (aired January 21, 2023).

she denied the charge laid against her. She was then tortured and abused, mentally, physically, and sexually, until she eventually confessed. Her so-called "confession" listed fifty-nine other people who were witches in her area, and so began in earnest the witch hunts in Britain by the church. Agnes Sampson was strangled and then burned at the stake at Castlehill on January 28, 1591. It's said that her ghost roams the Palace at Holyroodhouse still.

Agnes's tale is a tragic one; her only crime was trying to heal people through the traditions and practices that she had learned from her father. While these specific practices are not documented, Agnes Sampson is still a figure to remember as the first of the cunning folk to be prosecuted and killed under the new system of the growing radical wing of the church. This movement invested in politics and power began a reign of terror on local healers, midwives, and cunning folk in general that was to last for hundreds of years. It is thought that around 2,500 people died in England and Scotland by these witch hunts, and most of them were women.

Isobel Gowdie

Isobel Gowdie is another Scottish woman that was accused of Witchcraft in 1662. She lived in Lochloy with her husband, who was a tenant farmer. Her trial is perhaps the most famous (or infamous) of the Scottish witch trials, in which grand accounts of her doings were recorded by those who interrogated her. Some of these accounts seem exceptionally fanciful, which could be the visions induced by ergotism (an affliction caused by ergot, which is a mould that grows on rye; if eaten, it can induce hallucinations). It could be a remembrance and practice which remained from a more shamanistic bent from earlier traditional practices. It could also be the result of the vivid imaginations of those who questioned her, brought on and answered by asking leading questions. It could also be a combination of all of the above.

It may be that Isobel Gowdie's confessions are responsible for much of what we see today in modern Witchcraft. For example, she spoke about a witches' coven as having thirteen members, something that some modern-day covens, especially in Wicca, aim to achieve or describe to be the maximum number that is workable in a group setting.[8] Isobel made four confessions in total, beginning with meeting the devil at the local church at night. There is the usual statement of having intercourse with the devil, where his semen was described as "cold as spring well-water." I only mention this because in the subsequent confession of a fellow local witch, Janet Broadhead, she too describes the sexual act and the semen specifically as being "cold as spring well-water." To me, this indicates that the people investigating are asking leading questions in order for the responses to be almost identical. In many of these confessions, the practices to become a witch are almost word-for-word alike. This should make all readers of these confessions suspicious of the contents of the confessions and the methods by which they were acquired, to say the least. Read them with a grain or even a bucket of salt if necessary.

What is perhaps the most interesting of Isobel's confessions are the details of her working with the faeries, something which is little attested to, if at all, in subsequent confessions by other accused witches. This could be a remnant of a much older tradition of Faery Craft, which is often seen in the Celtic diaspora. Isobel describes meeting the queen and king of Faery and what they wore, but that is all that has been transcribed. For some unknown reason, a large portion of her dealings with those of the Faery realms was not recorded, which may indicate that those questioning her felt this information was irrelevant or utterly fantastical (unlike their fervent belief in the devil and his sexual longings), or it could even be information they thought was best kept hidden from the eyes of any who would read these confessions because it contained knowledge that they thought was best suppressed in order to live in a good Christian country (and which many locals might not find "evil" in the slightest). This gives us a hint as to

---

8 "Betwixt and Between: Isobel Gowdie, the Witch of Auldearn," Museum of Witchcraft and Magic Boscastle, https://museumofwitchcraftandmagic.co.uk /exhibitions/betwixt-and-between-isobel-gowdie-the-witch-of-auldearn-2 (accessed January 26, 2023).

a possible pre-Christian Faery tradition that existed in the area—a remnant of an older faith. Therefore, the confessions of Isobel might have a ring of truth to them and not entirely be the fabrication of the accusers and torturers that held her. Sadly, we will just never know for sure.

Isobel's confessions contain magical charms to shapeshift, raise the winds, call on the spirits or witch's familiars, create elfshot (a term used to describe a sudden pain or illness in humans or cattle through working with the faery folk), fly on a broom, heal (in the name of certain saints and the Holy Trinity), steal from farmers and fisherman, make a person ill or cause death, and combat the powers of Witchcraft, such as reversing a bewitchment upon a person.[9] Isobel's charm for riding a broom is an especially important piece of information for many practitioners of Witchcraft today. It speaks to many of a form of astral travel or even of hedge riding. For those who walk or perhaps even fly between the worlds, her account of flying and the spoken charm that she used is still important to this day. Once again, it could derive from the imaginings of her captors and torturers or it could be an actual practice; we simply do not know for certain. For many modern-day witches and hedge riders, however, it certainly rings true and has inspired many in their own practice (minus the whole devil bit). Her charm for spirit flight was thus:

> When I wish to take flight or to be far away, I take wild straw or bean-stalks and put them betwixt our feet and say thrice: horse and hattock, in the Devil's name! Or we would say thrice: horse and hattock, horse and go, horse and pellatris, ho ho![10]

A hattock is a small hat. Pellatris might be a variation of *pellatis*, which comes from the Latin *pello*, meaning to push, impel, or move forward (think of the pedal of a bicycle or even *peloton*, the main pack of cyclists in a race). Here we have the image of a witch with a hat riding a makeshift broom of sorts through the air. There have been a few recorded images of witch's riding brooms in early medieval texts; however, this is the first in a

9 Mills, *The Black Book of Isobel Gowdie*, 19–42.
10 Ibid., 68.

documented confession. So, next time you see that image anywhere, give a nod to old Izzy!

All in all, forty-one people were arrested after Isobel's confessions. Whether Isobel was killed after her confessions remains unknown, although most academics think that it is most likely she was, like many witches before her, found guilty of the crimes confessed and subsequently strangled and killed.[11]

Biddy Early

Biddy (Bridget) Early was an Irish woman from County Clare who was born in the late eighteenth century. It is said that she learned her skills from her mother, Ellen Early. She had a relationship with the faeries from a very early age, and some even say that she, her brother, and her son were "away with the fairies" and "changelings" (switched at birth with faery children by the faeries). She was orphaned at an early age, and therefore was very poor until she married her first husband. The couple lived in Feakle, and that is where her reputation began for her knowledge in the healing arts.

Biddy never charged money for her services; she preferred gifts such as food or alcohol, which was also used as a draw for local folk to come by her place of residence and have a good time. She was widowed early in life, as her first husband was quite a bit older than she was, and she remarried—to her own stepson! Her second husband developed a liver ailment (funny that, with all the booze going around), and so at the age of forty-two Biddy was widowed again. She remarried a much younger man, a fellow native of County Clare. They lived in a little cottage by a lake: Carter's Lough (sometimes called Kilbarron Lake), which later became known to some as Biddy Early's Lake. The water from her well supposedly had magical, curative powers.

It is said that Biddy was given a blue bottle by the faeries (or by the ghost of her dead son, Tom), and it was from this bottle that she expanded her powers. She was able to divine the future as well as see potential clients who were on their way to meet her; she was able to go out and meet them

11 Levack, *The Witchcraft Sourcebook*, 283.

halfway. Through the use of her bottle, she was also able to see what led the faeries to afflict people, such as the cursing of an entire herd of cows after the farmer had planted a whitethorn (hawthorn) bush along a fairy road.

She was an outspoken woman who often criticised and acted against the wishes of the Catholic priests in her area as well as the tenant farmers. She also stood up to the priests who would chastise her, such as a curate from Tipperary whom she "froze" in the saddle before he got to her cottage. (She later released him with a charm using blades of grass and invoking the Holy Trinity.[12]) It's likely that she caught the ire of the priests and doctors who were shunned in favour of her, due not only to her skill but also to the lack of money that changed hands. The people saved money by visiting Biddy. The owner of her cottage, a Doctor Murphy, eventually managed to evict her from her cottage after an unsuccessful attempt involving the local police, who were said to be rooted to the spot with her words and unable to carry out their orders. When the eviction finally took place, Biddy was sent to the poorhouse. Doctor Murphy's house in Limerick soon burned down with him inside it, even after she had warned him several times.

It is said that on her death, her blue bottle was thrown into the lake so that it could go back to the faeries. Some say that the attendant priest who gave her the last rites was the one to throw the bottle back into the lake. Her funeral was well attended by parishioners and clergy alike.

Biddy's work once again shows us that there is a connection between the faeries and practitioners of the magical arts. Many Celtic areas saw working with the faeries not as something evil, but as part of their life as it had always been. It's also a good demonstration of the personal independence that can be seen in many of the cunning folk, who aren't afraid to go against the grain.

---

12 *History Ireland Magazine*, "Feakle's Biddy Early."

Moll Pitcher

Famed for her fortunetelling abilities, the "world-renowned pythoness of Lynn," Moll Pitcher, lived in Lynn, Massachusetts. It is said that she came from a long line of magical practitioners.[13] She was born around 1736, the granddaughter of "the Wizard of Marblehead," Captain John Diamond. Captain Diamond had a magical ability to save sailors from drowning as well as find lost objects. Moll was often depicted as a haggard, elderly lady; however, other reports describe her as quite beautiful, and her descendants are "among the prettiest ladies of Lynn."

Many a sailor would refuse to sail because Moll had made a prediction that a shipwreck would occur. She prophesied for both the lower and upper classes and had a wide range of clientele. She read tea leaves by swirling them around in the cup, then tipping it upside down onto the saucer. Judging from the various positions of the leaves, she deduced what people wanted to know.

On July 12, 1879, the *Boston Traveler* published an extensive article that not only celebrated Moll but also tried to debunk the stories around her various talents. It made claims that her daughter helped her out by asking questions of those who came to her beforehand while Moll listened in an adjacent room, as well as her daughter employing some scare tactics, such as dragging a chain across the floor in an upper room when Moll threatened that the devil would be after those clients who wouldn't pay the price she asked.

George Pickingill

A cunning man from Essex, England, George Pickingill was born at the turn of the nineteenth century and lived quite a long life. He was quite famous (or infamous) in his day, and he still is in many Witchcraft circles today. Locally, he was known as "the Wise Man of Canewdon."[14]

George was possibly most known for his power to control animals and may have been part of a secret society of horse whisperers, known locally

13 Legends of America, "Moll Pitcher."
14 Howard, *East Anglian Witches and Wizards*, 114.

as "the Horseman's Word." He could calm or stop horses in their tracks and get stubborn and unwilling horses to move. He always walked with a blackthorn staff, which was called his "blasting rod." He could blast or paralyse people or animals with it, it is said, and he also threatened to harm farm machinery. Local farmers would bribe him with alcohol to keep him away. He could also heal minor wounds and stop the flow of blood, as well as find lost or stolen property.

Pickingill is perhaps most famous for being a "master of witches." It is said that he fathered many covens of witches in the area (around nine) and could summon a gathering of them by blowing his special silver whistle. Pickingill may have come from a hereditary line of witches. There is debate as to whether he was a major influence on the likes of Aleister Crowley and Gerald Gardner.[15]

• • •

This is just a brief example of the various cunning folk that lived in England and beyond. We can see some similarity between examples, such as a possible connection to an older Faery Craft or tradition of working with the faeries. There is also a connection to animals and the animal world, whether that is of a shapeshifting nature or an ability or affinity of working with animals. As well, we see abilities to both heal and harm, as well as locating lost objects and other forms of divination. Each of the above examples were about people who stood out in their community, perhaps unwittingly, but noticeably were different from the others in the area. They used their talents and abilities in a manner that was not only true to their nature and their own experiences, but also helped them survive in the world. That some were tortured and killed for it is deeply saddening; however, we can keep their names and their stories alive through research and remembrance. Though some would not have wanted to be connected to any Witchcraft of any kind, we can at least embrace their skills and talents for the wise women and men—the cunning folk—that they were.

15 Hutton, *The Triumph of the Moon*, 293.

Exercise

Why not try to find a local wisewoman or man, one of the cunning folk, from the history of your own local area? A quick search online or in the local library might lead to a wonderful journey ahead. You may even be very lucky if there are contemporary practitioners today that you can talk to and who may lead you onto a new path of investigation in your search for history. Local talks, pub moots, and metaphysical shops are great places to find information on local people involved in the craft, both past and present. If you can't find anything locally, try widening the search to your county, province, or state. You may be surprised at what you can find! You may find historical practitioners of the arts who were influenced by indigenous peoples of the area or have a culmination of various traditions imported from around the world. Investigate these as much as you can, for it may lead you down powerful paths of your own ancestry and heritage. Most importantly, read actively. With any book you read, write down notes in your journal or use a voice recorder to gather your thoughts on certain aspects, retain important quotes, and make the process of reading one of learning.

Armed with a printout of "Walking with Witches," my husband and I arrive in Mistley, near Manningtree, Essex. We begin by the old pub, the White Hart, where local legend has it that the Witchfinder General, Matthew Hopkins, met accusers. A slight shiver runs through me as the barest hint of anger and moral panic wafts through my mind.

We then progress to the tiny village green where four local women were hanged for Witchcraft. I stand in that place as a witch in the modern day and honour their memory, whether or not they themselves were actually witches. Woman to woman, I feel their persecution in my bones and in my spirit memory. With tears blurring my eyes, I read aloud their names: Anne West of Lawford, Helen Clark of Manningtree, Marian Hocket from Ramsey, Anne Cooper from Great Clacton.

We later pass the remains of the building where the self-styled Witchfinder General preached his sermons. I pass quickly by, a feeling of unease within me; so many so-called pious people willing to do harm to their fellow humans. We move on to the pond by Hopping Bridge, where it is most likely that the accused were "swum" or "dunked" in a predetermined attempt to prove their innocence or guilt. If they drowned, they were deemed innocent; if they floated and survived, they were guilty.

We pass by the Gamekeepers Pond, where the ghost of Matthew Hopkins is said to haunt. I feel nothing, which is just as well because I would have more than a few choice words to say to him should I come across his spirit. We go on to try and find the place where he was buried, but all that remains is the ruined

pieces of the church and no marked graves to speak of in the overgrown churchyard. Fitting, I think, but also a pity, as I would have liked to dance on his grave. That he lies in an unkempt, overgrown, unmarked grave in a place little visited is poetic justice, at the very least.

We then process to Old Knobbley, an ancient oak tree more than 800 years old. This tree was old during the witch hunts in the area, and who knows what happened beneath its gnarled and twisted branches. I spend time walking around the tree widdershins, its massive trunk so big it would take at least ten people linking their hands to encompass it. I sit with the tree for a while, listening to its stories, and then we make our way back to the village.

These are just some of the many stories in my part of the world, and there are so many to yet be discovered. I am thankful that the history is here and the stories are now being told, names are remembered, and the atrocities of those who accused the folk are laid bare for all to see. In the warm summer sunshine as the hawks soar high overhead in the green fields of Mistley, it is a blend of anger and injustice combined with peace and hope for a better world.

Chapter 2

The Hedge Witch Tradition

I have a new definition of a Witch: A Witch
is someone who is paying attention, who is
aware of the Divine Presence in all things.

. . . .

Phyllis Curott, *Witch Crafting*

In the previous chapter, we looked at some of the cunning folk from the past. Now let's take a look at what it means to be a hedge witch today. What sets this tradition of the craft apart from others? What are the major themes, what does the bulk of the work consist of, and why is it practiced? Some of these topics were touched upon in my previous book, but here we will take a closer look at the heart of the hedge witch tradition.

The hedge witch tradition rests on a foundation of three things: a deep love and respect for the natural world, the ability to work on your own, and a desire to walk between the worlds. Let's look at each of these in more detail.

Love and Respect for Nature

The hedge witch is inspired by, communes with, and is an integral part of their environment. In the daily occurrences in nature, the hedge witch finds ways in which they can live their lives in accordance with the cycles of the seasons. They take their cue from the flora and fauna around them, from the weather and the cycles of the sun and moon. They know when to be wild and when to be calm. They know when to express and when to turn inward. They know where the sunshine warms the earth and where the coolest shade can be found. They know the flows of streams, rivers, and seas around them and what lies in the earth beneath their feet. They listen to the songs of the birds and hear the changes in the song that herald the start of a new season, a new way of being. They listen to the cooing of the pigeons in a downtown park, the bark of a fox in a city suburb, and the call of a stag on a wild, windy heath.

The key is to spend time with nature, with your own local environment in particular. When you do this, you begin to understand how it works, how it all flows from one moment to the next. It's much easier to concentrate your practice on your own local patch, and it just makes more sense as that is the area in which you spend most of your time. Whether you are in a city or out in the rural countryside, there are cues and hints from nature that can show you how you fit in, where you fit in, and how you can contribute to the area's overall well-being.

I've lived both in the heart of cities and in the country. While I have a great aversion to cities, I learned how to cope and find the magic in those places where I needed to in order to keep the magic alive in my own soul and feel a connection to the natural world around me. It is so much easier for me out in the countryside, for sure. Others may have a very different experience.

In a city I would seek out any green space available near me. Sometimes this was just the small churchyard in the heart of a downtown area. There are usually some green spaces around churches where people have been buried. In these green spaces, you can find flora and fauna if you just look hard enough. From worms, beetles, and ants to birds, moles, and more, you can literally see that life flourishes upon the cycles of death and rebirth. The soil is literally made up of dead things: animals and plants that have rotted down and provide the rich earth where new life can begin again. In the heat of a hot summer day in the city centre, being able to sit on the grass in the shade of a stone church building can connect you to these cycles. In Britain and other places around the world, churches were often built upon sites of earlier Pagan worship, so you can also connect to the ancestors and the past through these places. Most cities usually have some parks and green spaces that are free to visit and roam, or even botanical gardens or arboretums that you can visit (sometimes for a fee). You can often become a member of these more formal spaces, which will save you money rather than paying upon each visit and which also contributes to a more financially secure base for them to operate. If money is an issue, see if there is a volunteer programme that you can join in return for free entry to the gardens.

Many cities are also built near local bodies of water, such as New York or Montreal, Boston or London, Copenhagen or Paris. Water is an important, life-giving element that we need to respect. Being around and with the water, forming a relationship with it and listening to the stories it has to tell can greatly inform us in our own way of being. Working to help keep it clean is an active way of giving back for the gifts of water in our own locality. Many cities have clean-up days along shorelines or rivers. A friend of mine combines her love of paddleboarding with a litter pick-up crew that gathers several times a month for Planet Patrol (formerly Plastic Patrol), cleaning up waterways across the UK.[16]

Wherever you are, visit farmers markets, learn what food is in season, and try to eat in accordance. Or see if there is a CSA or veg box scheme that you can order from, where local, seasonal fruit and veg (usually organic) are delivered to your door. Seek out places where you can buy organic food, preferably without plastic packaging. More and more shops have a "bring your own container" policy where you can fill up on the essentials by having bulk items that can be dispensed into your own containers. Items like rice, pasta, lentils, spices, and so much more can be found at these places. Many also have a refill scheme for household products too.

With regards to respecting nature, your personal hygiene products are also an important factor, not only to your own personal health but to the

16 https://planetpatrol.co.

health of the planet as a whole. Try to opt for plastic-free items. This means not only items that aren't in a plastic container, but items that don't have microplastics in them. At the time of writing this book, I was amazed at how much microplastics are in almost every shampoo, face cleanser, body moisturiser, shower gel, bubble bath, and makeup product. While microbeads have been banned for some time, there are now "strings" or polymers of plastic that are found in almost every product. Some of the main culprits in the ingredients list are dimethicone, polyethelene, acrylates copolymer, polyquaternium (as of writing this is still under debate as a "sceptical microplastic, but probably best to avoid until certain"), and carbomer. These legal microplastics are everywhere: look out for anything that has *acrylic* or *acrylate* in the word, or a synthetic polymer of any kind. Some companies such as UpCircle in the UK use only natural ingredients (many of which are upcycled and saved from food industry waste), in glass bottles and jars that you can refill through the mail and for which you will receive a sizeable discount in the process.[17] How wonderful is that?

Clothing is another part of being conscious of the planet's welfare. So much clothing now consists of plastic microfibers that flow into our water systems with every wash. Cotton clothing uses so much water and pesticides that you really have to be careful in buying products with a sustainable cotton process. Even bamboo, which is a wonderful plant for fabric, can often undergo an environmental nightmare when processed into viscose. Investigating and reading up on all this is time-consuming and, quite frankly, depressing. The best and most sustainable thing you can do is buy the bulk of your clothing secondhand and commit to "no buy" years where you only replace the essential items that have worn out and cannot be mended.[18]

A love of and respect for nature is not just admiring beautiful sunsets, going for long walks, and meditating on the cycles of life. It is also about a

---

17 https://upcirclebeauty.com.
18 A great YouTube channel for more on how to make the most of your wardrobe and buy secondhand is Use Less: https://www.youtube.com/@UseLess_dk (accessed February 1, 2023).

very real and active way of living and being in the world that reflects your love and dedication to a better relationship with the natural world. Find out new and different ways that you can connect to the natural world and its rhythms, how you can show your love and devotion to this planet we call home, and how that reflects your own practice as a hedge witch. Incorporate the beauty with the practicality of living, of walking your talk and integrating fully the lessons that nature has to teach us. As Phyllis Curott said,

> We make the best magic in Nature because Nature makes the best magic. Nature is magic, because it is the body of the Divine. And Nature's magic doesn't have to be imagined, it just has to be experienced.[19]

An Ability to Work Alone

Working as a hedge witch is, by and far, a solitary tradition. Though you may sometimes gather together with friends to celebrate a certain sabbat or esbat, on the whole your work is done by yourself. All the learning, all the practice, and all the wisdom gained is something that you must take on for yourself. It can be difficult for those who require some pressure to keep up with their work to walk this path alone. It is a path of self-discipline as well as self-love. We have to be hard enough with ourselves so that we do not allow our path to become more of a hobby than a spiritual practice, but we must also remember that no one is perfect and that we can and will fail occasionally in maintaining our standards. We will go through glorious peaks and valleys in our practice, moments of pure ecstasy, joy, and true connection, and other times of dullness and withdrawal.

There will be dormant periods in your life and in your practice where some of your practices may take a back seat as you readjust to your new worldview. For myself, there are times where I just need a break from everything—a couple of weeks where I can reset myself and restore factory settings so I can start anew with fresh eyes. If there is a dormant period in

19 Curott, *Witch Crafting*, 71.

your practice, do not despair. Do the simple things and reconnect fully when it is time.

There is a certain stillness and quietness that is often required in this path. When we are alone, we learn how the silence and stillness can be our greatest teachers. Only by being quiet ourselves can we hear the songs and stories of the natural world around us. We have to be okay with this silence, with being alone with ourselves. Wiccan author Thorn Mooney once wrote:

> If there were no one to tell, no one to validate you, and no one to offer instant feedback, what would your Witchcraft look like? Who are you when you are alone with your spirits, your gods, your self?[20]

Being alone is something that many people are struggling with in our modern world. I can't remember the last time I saw someone standing in a queue or sitting in a restaurant alone (or even with others) who wasn't on their phone. It seems that the majority of people today have forgotten how to be alone, even for the merest of minutes. We have to learn how to separate ourselves from our devices, handy though they may be, and simply pay attention.

There is no one who can walk this path for you. You may find guides along the path, but it's up to you to pick up your feet and find your own way. You have to discover who you are both as a person and as a witch.

A Desire to Walk Between the Worlds

Hedge Witchcraft has, at its core, an ecstatic practice of hedge riding. You must familiarise yourself with different ways of reaching that ecstatic state, ways that work for you. Some people may try to put forward that there are only certain and specific ways to reach that ecstatic state, but I strongly disagree. We are each so very different, with our own life's experiences behind and before us, that the way we approach our hedge riding tradition will vary greatly. How I ride the hedge will be different from how you perform

20 Mooney, "Winter Calls for Silence."

the work because of everything that I have learned and the life that I have lived. Hedge riding and all trance practices are unique to the individual.

This doesn't mean that we can't find ways into our own practice. In my previous book, I gave several ways of reaching that trance state, and I will provide more later on in this work. You can follow my suggestions and then use them as guidelines to how you are going to get yourself to that ecstatic space between the worlds.

Hedge riding does indeed define the tradition of Hedge Witchcraft. If there isn't a trance or ecstatic element to parts of your work, if you aren't riding the hedge to the otherworld, then you are most likely practicing something different, such as Green Witchcraft, if labels must be applied. Riding the hedge and walking between the worlds is something that you must really want to do in order to learn more and bring more wisdom into this world, your practice, and your own being.

Exercise

Journal your thoughts on these three aspects of Hedge Witchcraft: love and respect for nature, the ability to work alone, and the desire to walk between the worlds. Take some time with each section, really going into detail about how you feel regarding each aspect and what you can do to go deeper into each one. Writing it out helps solidify it in your mind, just as speaking aloud puts your thoughts and desires out into the world and makes them come alive. If you find writing difficult, then record your thoughts using a digital or analogue recording device. Most mobile phones have built-in voice recorders that you can use to gather your thoughts. Don't skip this part; you can't do it all in your head.

I walk out onto the heath, my drum in its bag and a goal in my mind. I take the time to connect to the spirits of the land around me, to listen and pay attention to what is going on this day on the heath. I find a special spot and take some more time to commune with the energy of the day and listen to the woodpeckers and the cries of the hawks soaring high overhead on the thermals. I leave an offering of seeds for the deer and badgers, squirrels and foxes. I sit in silence, centring in myself and then out into the wider landscape. Once I am ready, I pull out my drum and breathe lightly upon it, waking it up and connecting it to my soul. I softly drum and sing into the spring sunshine, letting the sounds carry me between the worlds. I see the world tree before me, and soon I am hedge riding out into the realm of the otherworld, seeking what it is that I need to bring back into this world.

And all around me the sun shines and the quiet stillness of nature guides me deeper.

Chapter 3

Folklore and Working with the Land

One of the best things about folklore and
fairy tales is that the best fantasy is what you
find right around the corner, in this world.
That's where the old stuff came from.

· · · · · ·

Terri Windling

Folklore is often a repository for stories of the land itself and the beings that inhabit it. It is important, therefore, to understand and explore the folklore of the area where you live. Whether it's a city or the suburbs, the rural countryside or a small town, there are always stories to find hidden both in history and the landscape itself.

There is always folklore, the knowledge of the ways of the land, wherever you live. Some of this folklore might be new, say from the last fifty years or so, and some of it might be older or even ancient. What we must remember is that age does not equal validity. Just because someone said or thought something two thousand years ago doesn't make it right or even appropriate for today. That being said, knowledge of the old ways can help us understand where we are in the present moment and bring a connection to the past that helps us move forward armed with knowledge and the experience of our ancestors. Equally, newer folklore doesn't mean it isn't relevant or important. We can connect to the land at any stage in our human evolution, and the stories that we bring back from that connection can have great meaning, helping others connect more fully.

Here in Britain, there is much folklore about the Fair Folk, otherwise known as faeries. Similar beings exist all over the world in varying forms. Some believe that they represent aspects of nature and operate as spirits of plants or a physical natural location such as a river, glen, or waterfall. Others see these beings as otherworldly dwellers whose paths cross ours every now and then, for even as we are able to travel to the otherworld, so are they able to travel to this world, and probably with more skill. How you view these beings is completely reliant upon your experience of them. You can read all about them in books and journals and listen to the local tales told of them in your area, but only through direct experience will you be able to make a sound judgement.

Many books may tell you that the beings of the otherworld are dangerous and should be treated with caution. These cautionary tales may be completely justified or the product of the Christianisation of the land, turning what was once a being one could work with to a demon or other kind of fiend from hell. It's impossible to tell which material is coming from a Pagan perspective and which is coming from a Christian perspective, and most likely it is an amalgamation of the two. Again, only direct experience will bring you to a real understanding.

Folklore from a Local Area

Where I live in Suffolk, we have in our local folklore a being called Black Shuck. It is described as a huge black dog with glowing red eyes, often seen on the heathland and appearing out of the mist. It is also seen in the in-between places such as crossroads, parish boundaries, river edges, fenland, cliff edges, and church graveyards. In my local area, it's said that if you see Black Shuck walking directly toward you, a death (your or someone you love) is coming soon, but if you see it walking beside or parallel to you from a distance, it is protecting you.

The most famous Black Shuck sighting in the UK occurred just down the now A12 highway from where I live on the Suffolk Coast. During a vicious thunderstorm on August 4, 1577, a huge black hound attacked the Blythburgh Church and supposedly killed many parishioners, even leaving its claw marks on the north church door where it still can be seen to this day. It then went on to attack another church nearby in Bungay. There is a black dog that haunts the coastline at Leiston, known as Galley Trot. The bones of a huge dog were discovered in an archaeological dig at Leiston Abbey in 2013, where it was conjectured that the dog was 7 feet in length and weighed around 200 pounds. This made all the local papers, declaring that the bones of Black Shuck had been found! In nearby Melton there is another Galley Trot, a white spectral hound that haunts the site of the old toll gates. A large dog haunts the ruins of Greyfriars Monastery, part of the abbey ruins in the town of Dunwich, which is falling into the sea due to coastal erosion from the Middle Ages onward. In the neighbouring county of Lincolnshire to my home region of East Anglia, there are reports of a large dog that guarded and protected ladies who had to make their way home on their own.

Though I have never seen Black Shuck for myself, I really do feel him (it is always described as a "he") in the landscape as a being that crosses from the otherworld to this world when the need or desire takes him. The tales of Black Shuck harming beings seem a little too fantastic to me, and since they usually take place near or in churches, this makes them immediately suspect to me. The attack at Blythburgh Church was most likely lightning from a great storm striking the steeple. I feel that Black Shuck is a guardian spirit of the land, and it's best to make friends with him and the land as quickly and as best you can. He may also be the spirit of the wild, untamed forces of nature in our area, such as the great thunderstorms that are so rare here on the coast of the North Sea and which scared so many people during church services in Blythburgh and Bungay. He may be a manifestation of the spirit of the mists or the heathland or of roads and byways. Whatever Black Shuck is, as a hedge witch I feel that it is important to work with him and understand as much as I can about him and the natural world in which he operates.

Mermaids that drown children, captured faeries whose death means disaster, ghosts of all kinds: all these and more are tales from my local area. Researching these tales with a Pagan point of view can lead to interesting finds, such as holy wells, how to treat the land you farm, reconnecting with the past, and altering the conception of linear time. Most of the recorded tales were told and written down from a Christian perspective, so they bear a large bias toward anything "supernatural." It is up to us to discover if a being from the otherworld truly means us harm or whether by reading between the lines of these cautionary tales we might find ways to honour these spirits and work with them to bring about a beneficial relationship for both parties.

Where I grew up in Quebec, Canada, there is an interesting Quebecois tale of the Maudite (the damned). It's a tale that, upon reflection, may be indicative of astral travel or even hedge riding. A group of loggers far away from home on a cold winter's night made a pact with the devil to take them home for a New Year's Eve celebration. They missed their families dearly and would have done anything to be with them for this night, so they called upon the devil to create a *chasse galerie*, a canoe that could fly them home. There were conditions: they could not swear, drink, wear religious symbols, or perform symbolic acts, and they must be back before dawn. They agreed, hopped into the large canoe, and flew home to their loved ones. They had a grand old time. As the night drew on and dawn approached, they gathered back in the canoe. They had to tie up and gag the cook and throw him in the bottom of the canoe, for he was as drunk as a skunk and swore like a sailor. However, the problem was that the cook was the only one who knew how to steer this magical canoe, so it began to swerve left, then right, then all over the place. The men began to swear, and one made the sign of the cross in fear. It was then that the canoe hit a tall tree (or a church steeple, depending on who is telling this tale) and all the men fell out. These men are forever doomed to fly their canoe through hell, coming out once a year to ride the night skies on New Year's Eve.[21]

---

21 There's even a beer named after this tale from a brewery in Quebec. See the video and hear the legend here: "Maudite—About the Legend," https://youtu.be /CFt0ZhZGA0g (accessed February 28, 2023).

This tale has some similarities with the Wild Hunt folklore of Europe, who some say are doomed souls that must ride the wintery skies in penance. Like so many other tales, there is a pact made with the devil in order for the powers to be available, but we can see parallels in establishing a relationship with the land, the spirits of the land, and beings from the otherworld in our own hedge riding practice. As well, it's probably always better not to drink or swear when doing this work. Respect for all beings is essential.

With the internet, it is even easier to research local folklore. Many amateur folklorists, as well as academics, put up their findings on all sorts of sites. This can be a great jumping-off point for your own pursuit of the local traditions and tales of your area. Links to books are often referenced, and a visit to your local library can round it out nicely. If there is a local folklore club in your area, even better! There might be pub moots you can attend or folklore societies that have monthly gatherings. Other local Pagans might have an ear to the ground of likely groups, as this is of interest to many who walk this path. I know local Morris dancers and Saxon reenactors who have led me down some interesting routes of research!

Stories are so very important to humanity. It's how we have passed on knowledge for thousands of years. Stories grow, change and evolve even as we do, showing that a relationship to a story is a fluid one. So too is our relationship to the land. As we learn more, as we grow, our relationship to the land will change hopefully for the better. We will learn how to work more closely with it, and perhaps even find new tales to tell and pass on to future generations. These tales are not fantasy, but relate our experiences with the land and with the other-than-human inhabitants that live alongside us, both from this world and the otherworld.

Working with the Land

Working with the land where you live will certainly bring you into contact with many other-than-human beings, both of this world and the otherworld. This might happen in the physical, but it may also happen when performing a hedge riding. By researching your local folklore, you may find traditional ways that people worked with the land and thereby either re-create them or come up with newer ways that are more relevant and appropriate to our modern time. Where I live, it's traditional to leave a corner of a field wild, often called the Devil's Plantation, as an offering to "the devil" (or local land spirits, more likely). We are now understanding the importance of leaving a wild patch in our gardens and how that increases and benefits the local wildlife. Having perfectly manicured lawns kept with pesticides and herbicides isn't a very good idea if one is to follow the hedge witch tradition. Learning what grows locally, what needs boosting, and how you can accomplish this within your means is something that is very important to consider.

Leave a wild patch if you own a garden. Plant local flowers that will attract bees and other pollinating insects. Garden organically. Work with the land to understand what grows well in your area and what doesn't thrive. In our sandy loam on the edge of the heathland, close to the North Sea, we are limited as to what grows well in the soil around our home. But by paying attention to the land around us, we can see what works well and also experiment with great success.

If all you have is a window box, then use that! Grow flowers for the bees and herbs for your kitchen. Hang a birdfeeder on your balcony. Adopt a run-down, derelict area in your neighbourhood and make it a space where it can benefit everyone, human and nonhuman. Start up community gardens. Sign up for an allotment where you can grow your own flowers or food.

Visit local museums. Most towns will have small museums, especially here in Britain. In my part of England, many of these are agricultural museums. These can teach us how the land was worked in earlier times, help us learn from previous mistakes and lack of knowledge, and perhaps reconnect to traditional ways that further us in our own hedge witch practice.

Look to the local landscape. Rivers, valleys, mountains—all these usually have a story or at least a name attached to them that might lead you to indigenous history or a colonial past. Visit these places with a hedge witch's perspective and open yourself to the energies present. What do they tell you? What wishes to be honoured, to be worked with; what wishes to establish a relationship with you? What offerings are traditionally left there, and are they appropriate for you to leave today? Perform a hedge riding at these places to connect on a deeper level to the beings around you, both the seen and the unseen. Allow them and the space to come to you, to talk to you. A hedge witch makes friends with the spirits of their local area.

Exercise

Go to your local library or research online some folklore from your area. What does it tell you about the land and how people lived and worked with the land? Is there any wisdom that can be gained from this knowledge that you can put into your own practice? What is the land itself telling you?

I walk along the beach, my husband having wandered ahead. It's a bright, sunny, glorious autumn day, yet there are very few people around. Vast stretches of sand lie before me, with large waves rolling onto the shore. We walk for an hour, with me falling behind again and again as I am lulled by the crashing sound of the waves. Suddenly there is pressure in my head and my vision shifts. I see a shadowy form walking toward me, a transparent, mist-like form. I strain my eyes to get a better look, and I can make out the form of a sailor. He is just walking along the beach as we are, but I know that he is not here as we are in corporeal form. There is a slight sadness attached to him, and then he disappears like the mist on a sunny day.

I stop and look around me. There is no one nearby. I look up to the cliffs and can see that we are near the small hamlet of Dunwich, which used to be a great town before the majority of it fell into the sea one dark and stormy night. I look out to the waves and listen closely to see if I can hear the church bells ringing under the water, but all I hear are the cries of gulls. I look ahead and see my husband, who has turned around and is waiting for me to catch up yet again.

Once home I turn on the computer and do a quick search online. Yes, there is a sailor ghost that walks the beaches, looking for his lost love who most likely perished in the great storm that swept away most of the town in 1286. Many have seen him striding with purpose on that stretch of coast.

I am reminded of our fragile relationship with the sea in this part of the world, and how we must work with everything that we have to keep our ocean levels where they are. Storm surges and rising seas are the biggest threats to our sandy coastline here in the east of England, and vast swathes of land are having to be abandoned by people due to coastal erosion, poor sea defences, and a government who refuses to meet climate change targets.

I walk down to the beach in my village that evening and say a prayer for Nehalennia, the goddess of the North Sea, asking her what more I can do in order to honour her and protect this part of the coast. She whispers her instructions softly in my ear through the rolling pebbles of shingle as each wave pulls them back into the sea.

Part 2
EXPERIENCE
Preparatory Work *for* Going Deeper

Chapter 4

Know Thyself

Wisdom is the recovery of innocence
at the far end of experience.

· · · · · · ·

David Bentley Hart, *The Experience
of God: Being, Consciousness, Bliss*

"Know thyself" is written at the entrance to the world-famous Temple of
Apollo at Delphi in Greece. This simple phrase contains so much meaning,
and in this chapter we will take a closer look at what it means to know
thyself and how to begin this understanding of our own self and our soul.

So why is it important to know thyself, and what does it have to do with
the craft of the hedge witch? Well, to begin with, we must first understand
ourselves; in doing so, we come to better understand others and the world
around us. Does this make us self-centred egomaniacs? Of course not. This
is a study of the self, not the glorification of the self. We must be prepared
to take a long, hard look at our way of being in the world, sometimes from
an emotive and sometimes from a detached perspective. We must look at
the good and the not-so-good aspects of ourselves, our behaviour, and our
tendencies. This means looking at the shadow aspects of ourselves to better
understand our triggers—and therefore better understand the root causes

of much of our behaviour—in order to function more efficiently, compassionately, and beneficially in our lives.

What Is the Self?

Doctors Freud and Jung came up with concepts of the self that are the most popular today. Most everyone is aware of the conscious mind and the subconscious mind. The conscious mind can be divided into two parts: the persona and the ego. The persona is the image we project to others; it is our "front." The persona can contain many different fronts, such as the person we are when we are at work, the person we are when we are playing rugby, the person we are when we visit our elderly parents in a care home, the person we are when we are on a night out with our friends—you get the idea. We all have many such masks that we wear in our everyday lives, and these masks change and develop through the years as we move from experience to experience.

What are the masks that you wear in your everyday life? Can you put these aside or are they an integral part of who you think you are? Are there masks that you don't currently wear but would like to? Is there any benefit to wearing a mask? Who is the person behind the mask?

The ego is what underlies the persona in that it is what we believe that we are, as opposed to what it is that we are pretending to be. We like to think many different things about ourselves, and we like to also not think many things about ourselves. There is a lot of ourselves that we ignore or would just rather not confront, so we create an image of ourselves that is incomplete. Courtney Carver, in her book *Project 333*, said a statement that really stopped me in my tracks: "How will you know the truth if you believe everything you think?"[22] If we rely solely on our ego to understand ourselves, we are only thinking about a piece of ourselves and not the whole truth of it. To understand the whole truth, we need to look at the shadow.

22 Carver, *Project 333*, 45.

What Is the Shadow?

The shadow consists of the parts of the ego that we do not want to look at, understand, confront, or challenge. They can exist in both the conscious and subconscious aspects of our mind. We can wilfully ignore the shadow or not even know of its existence through a lack of personal introspection. Jung stated:

> The Shadow personifies everything that the subject refuses to acknowledge about himself and yet is always thrusting itself upon him directly or indirectly—for instance, inferior traits of character and other incompatible tendencies.[23]

Often the shadow arises when we are upset with other people. This upset is caused by the person reflecting personal traits we have within ourselves that we do not wish to confront or acknowledge. An example could look like this: say there is a person you know who really, really bugs you. Perhaps they are a drama queen and take over every situation they are in, making it all about themselves. This annoys you to no end. Why does this annoy you so much? Could it be that you see a part of yourself being reflected back at you, no matter how large or small a part it may be? Perhaps even a past self, a habit or custom that you now no longer engage with, that reminds you of who you used to be?

Other times the shadow is that which has been created out of an experience in the past that was used as a coping mechanism in order to help us survive a traumatic situation.[24] Grief, abuse, and accidents can all create such coping mechanisms that, when used in any other situation other than the original one, may not be conducive to being the best person you can be. These coping mechanisms can hinder your personal growth and so must be looked at deeply in order to understand your true self and come into your own personal sovereignty.

As an example, say you had a very bad experience with bullying. You can remember that person's face clearly. Now, two, ten, twenty years later, a

---

23 Jung, *The Collected Works*, 284–285.
24 Telyndru, *The Mythic Moons of Avalon*, 17.

new person in the office looks very similar to that person who bullied you in the past. You have a hard time even looking at this person, let alone talking to them. You do everything you can to avoid talking or working with this person, to the detriment of your work.

In another example, a dog chased you once when you were riding your bicycle. This was a big dog, and it bit your ankle. After that, you didn't want to be around any dogs in case they bit you. You created a fear of dogs based upon a single past experience.

In an example from my own experience, when I was bullied as a teenager, the adults around me would tell me that the bullies were just jealous of me and that I was much better than them. Indeed, jealousy may have been the reason I was bullied (I will never truly know), but the thinking that I was better than them stayed with me for a long time. For decades I believed that because they were the bullies and I was the one bullied, I was better than they were. I now understand that I am no better than they are, no better than anyone, and that this coping mechanism that helped me through a very difficult period in my life was no longer appropriate, even in situations where I was bullied as an adult.

Author Jhenah Telyndru works deeply with shadow aspects in all her work. In *Mythic Moons of Avalon*, she beautifully states:

> The issue with shadow tendencies is not that they exist within us at all, for in our times of greatest need they served a critically important role and could be seen as, perhaps, our greatest ally in those times of intense vulnerability. Problems arise when the compensatory behaviors and perspectives the shadow gifted us with have outlived the situations which birthed them . . . we unconsciously react to the old wound rather than the present moment. And that is the key: when we are anchored in past traumas that prevent us from seeing the present with clarity, we react rather than respond.[25]

We have to learn how to act with intention, coming from a place of clarity rather than living from a place of reaction, which is based on an unwillingness to be in the present moment truthfully. We have to be fully respon-

---

25 Telyndru, *The Mythic Moons of Avalon*, 18.

sible for our lives, ourselves, and how we live in the world. This means looking at aspects of the self that are less than pleasing or less than pleasant. Only then can we live intentionally, freed from past wounds while not forgetting them, so that we can truly turn our learning into wisdom.

Other Pagan Views of the Self

In some other traditions, there are different aspects of the self. The author Starhawk talks of Younger Self, Talking Self, and Deep Self, all of which derive from the Faery/Feri tradition. Here, Younger Self is that part of our psyche that communicates and understands through the senses and emotions; Talking Self is our everyday functioning self; and Deep Self is deity, which is immanent in everyone and everything.[26] Let's look at this a little more closely.

Younger Self is intuitive. It is also instinctive. It works with symbols, which makes it a huge part of the magical realm. When we are doing ritual, we are working with Younger Self through the imagery, pageantry, and symbolism that we are trying to create through the ritual in order to achieve our goal. Younger Self knows intuitively what is right and what isn't right for us, but it is more often than not overridden by Talking Self's logic.[27] When we are playing, imagining, being artistic, or working magic, we are mostly working with Younger Self. It is right brain all the way.

Talking Self is the grown-up, the voice of logic and reason. This is our left-brain thinking, the one that analyses and judges. It lives for ordinary reality and provides us with checks and balances when it comes to working with the Younger Self. Younger Self might want to go and hug that cute bear cub in the woods, but Talking Self reminds you that the mother may be around somewhere and will hurt you if you go near her cub.

Deep Self is accessed through Younger Self. Talking Self is too rational to deal with such things as deity, magic, ritual, and so on. It can take us through a ritual practically and safely, without setting ourselves alight by a candle or tripping over the altar. However, Talking Self does not reach

26 Starhawk, *The Spiral Dance*, 45.
27 Starhawk et al., *The Twelve White Swans*, 12.

the deity within ourselves. Younger Self understands that on a soul level, and so we entice Younger Self to help us establish a relationship and communicate with Deep Self through the things that Younger Self loves such as play, music, symbolism, and so on. Witchcraft is a tradition and way of being that operates on all levels. Knowing when to walk away from Talking Self to discover new worlds, new experiences, and connect with the divine (or whatever it is that we are seeking to connect with) is a whole other level that Talking Self just wouldn't understand. Talking Self is necessary for our survival, but we rely on it far too much in these modern times, and we need to reawaken our Younger Self in order to connect with our Deep Self.

Who we really are may be hidden beneath many layers of Talking Self's definitions, which, for the most part, have come to us from external sources. Seeking our true selves involves a return to Younger Self to find those missing pieces that are often a part of the shamanic practice of soul retrieval as we know it today. True healing comes from Deep Self, which is accessed through Younger Self. To find out more about these aspects of self, see Starhawk's *The Spiral Dance* (I recommend getting the twentieth-anniversary edition for its insights and commentary) as well as Starhawk and Hilary Valentine's *The Twelve White Swans: A Journey to the Realm of Magic, Healing, and Action.*

• • •

In some Pagan traditions such as Wicca, an exploration of the self and these aspects of the self is usually done through the three degrees of initiation. As a hedge witch, it is up to you to take responsibility for the entire journey of knowing thyself and in doing so coming into better harmony with the world around you. Only when we do not allow ourselves to get in the way can we truly move forward. There is so much ego, shadow, and lack of self-discipline in the world today. In order to understand and work with others (human and nonhuman), we need to understand ourselves fully, and this means looking at the bad parts of ourselves, what aspects we need to work on, what our triggers are, and how we can act with intention in the world instead of simply reacting to everything. We can work with Younger, Talking, and Deep Self through a newfound awareness of their being and establish clear lines of communication that benefit us on our journey toward true relationship with the self, others, and the natural world. At the end of this chapter are some questions to help get you started. But how can this knowledge create harmony with the world around us?

The Hero's Journey

We can best see how this newfound knowledge of ourselves can better our lives and create a deep integration with the world around us through what is known as "the hero's journey." In the stages of the journey, the hero leaves home, learns lessons, acquires new knowledge, and returns transformed. It is in this final stage of return where integration comes into play, which is where the real heart of the matter lies. In his work *The Hero with a Thousand Faces*, author Joseph Campbell states:

> A hero ventures forth from the world of common day into a region of supernatural wonder: fabulous forces are there encountered and a decisive victory is won: the hero comes back from this mysterious adventure with the power to bestow boons on his fellow man.[28]

As a hedge witch, you will be undertaking journeys not only in this world, but also in the otherworld. When riding the hedge, if we don't truly know who we are, we might come across aspects of ourselves in our working and not see them for what they are. We might bring fantasy elements into our hedge riding experiences, forgoing a true shift to the otherworld and instead only seeing or creating a story that we wish to see or participate in. Only when we understand ourselves can we perform really in-depth hedge riding without the constraints of those parts of our conscious and subconscious mind holding us back or keeping us in a state of self-denial. The craft of hedge riding depends largely on letting yourself go in order to bring wisdom back from the otherworld that you can use in your everyday life. These are the "boons" Campbell suggested.

---

28 Campbell, *The Hero with a Thousand Faces*, 23.

Integration

For the hedge witch, understanding the true self is not only empowering but also can bring other gifts or boons to their life, including a much deeper integration with the natural world around them. By understanding the self, we can then put aside the self for moments of true integration with our landscape. We can't put down what we don't know we're holding. When we're aware of all that we are, we can let that go as well in order to hear the songs of the spirits of nature all around us. We can work with the spirits of plants and truly hear what they are trying to tell us. We can practice divination without ourselves getting in the way of our work. We can craft our magic based upon a true knowledge of the self rather than wearing the masks of the persona or by simply focusing on the good parts that we want to present to others. Instead, our magic will be crafted through a thorough understanding of how we work, how our minds work and how our souls respond to the teachings.

Have you ever been in the song of a blackbird? Not just listening to a blackbird and thinking, "I hear the blackbird. What a nice song." Rather, this is becoming the song itself: becoming the blackbird, becoming the dusk that settles all around and causes the song to flow. It's a truly deep integration that can be achieved only by knowing yourself. When you know yourself, you can then let go of that self to experience a pure moment where there is no I or you or other.

Journal Prompts

- Who do you think you are?
- Who do you really think you are? Looking deeper, is there anything to add/subtract?
- Is it okay to have a "front"? Who is the person behind the mask, and what can they tell you?
- What past experiences have created coping mechanisms that no longer serve you?

- What is it about others that reflects your shadow back to you?

- Where have you simply reacted to a situation in the past, and where did you or could you have acted with intention? What do you suppose the outcome would be if you acted with intention in most situations?

- What is your Younger Self trying to tell you? How is your Talking Self overriding this on a daily basis? Can you truly find Deep Self within?

- How can you begin true, deep integration with your local landscape?

SUGGESTED READING

A Life of Meaning: Relocating the Centre of Your Spiritual Gravity by James Hollis (Sounds True Publishing, 2023)
We need to re-centre and find our focus and our own self every now and then, and this is a good guide on how to accomplish that in a well-written, thoughtful form.

Soul Shift: The Weary Human's Guide to Getting Unstuck and Reclaiming Your Path to Joy by Rachel Macy Stafford (Sounds True Publishing, 2023)
This book is a wonderful way to reconnect with your own self as well as help us find the joy and beauty that is all around us.

Through trance work and deep ritual, I begin to heal. I work with various goddesses who help me better understand myself. I lift my various masks and peer under them at the person beneath. Who is she? This work leads me deeper and deeper into the layers of my soul.

We all wear masks. This is what I come to realise. These masks are not necessarily a bad thing. They help us move forward, be brave, and fake it until we make it. They are our armour; they protect us and keep us safe until we are ready to lift them and show our true faces.

I journey to the White Spring in Glastonbury, and it is there I see a vision of the goddess Blodeuwedd rising out from the sacred pool. She is naked but for a cloak of white owl feathers, and she screams at me with her screech owl–like voice: "Choose the mask you want to wear or else others will choose it for you!" She collapses back as a waterfall into the pool, and all is still once more.

I write all this down in my journal, noting that the journey of the self is one that is never-ending.

Chapter 5

Working with Energy

With color one obtains an energy that
seems to stem from witchcraft.

· · · · · ·

Henri Matisse

Now that you have begun the work of better understanding your self, your motivations, and how you work in the world, we turn to an element of Witchcraft that is very important: working with energy. The reasons for working with energy are manifold; if we wish to cast a circle, we are working with energy. If we are doing spellcraft or herbcraft, we are working with energy. If we are hedge riding, we are working with energy. It's important to understand the nature of energy in Witchcraft and how we use it in our own work as a hedge witch.

What Is Energy and How Do We Work with It?

The world is made up of energy. Everything is energy—energy that is moving and flowing. A rock is energy. So is a tree, your cat, your mother. Albert Einstein with his famous equation of $E=mc^2$ showed the world that mass and energy are fluid and can be changed into each other, whereas previously they were thought of as two distinct and separate entities.

As such, we can work with different forms of energy, including our own. We can raise energy, lower energy, blend energy, send it out and take it in, or work to keep it in balance. This is what many spiritual practices are all about. We can learn to work with our own energy first and foremost, just as we have learned more about ourselves in the previous chapter. In doing so, we will understand the energy of other things as well and see that the edges where two things meet are fluid and changeable. As such, we can work with energy in our Hedge Witchcraft and achieve whatever goal it is that we have set ourselves.

In her book *Intuitive Witchcraft*, Astrea Taylor discusses the four types of energy that we, as witches, can work with: physical energy, emotional energy, mental energy, and spiritual energy.[29] She likens these types of energy to Maslow's hierarchy of needs, represented as a pyramid from which our most base needs require to be met before we can move on to other needs. In Taylor's work, she uses the witch's hat instead of a pyramid (love it) and shows how we need to work up from physical energy to the topmost part of the hat: spiritual energy. Each type of energy affects the other, and so we need to work from a secure base of physical energy before we can explore and work with the others.

Keeping ourselves in good physical condition will certainly affect our physical energy levels. I know that if I don't eat right or haven't exercised for days, I feel lethargic. It affects my emotional, mental, and spiritual energy as well, making them feel out of sorts and disconnected. So I exercise regularly, not only for my physical well-being but also my emotional, mental, and spiritual well-being.

My emotional energy also needs to be kept in balance. As an empath, situations that other people can brush off or simply ignore will really upset me, throw me off, or push me away. From watching the nightly news on television to being in a crowd of people, I have to guard my emotional energy from being tainted by what is happening around me, while still staying attuned to the world so that I can act with intention. It's not easy.

---

29 Taylor, *Intuitive Witchcraft*, chapter 2.

My mental energy is deeply affected by physical, emotional, and spiritual energy. To keep it balanced and able to provide me with what I need throughout each day, I have to take care to check in with myself. I do this through daily meditation and shorter time-outs—five or ten minutes to step aside and be alone (or with the cat), watch the sun set, listen to the birds, feel the sun on my face, etc.

My spiritual energy is kept in balance through my rituals, prayers, and meditations. Communing with the divine, opening my heart to beings of the spirit world, helps me recharge my batteries, keep the inspiration flowing, and give me hope each and every day.

We feel energy all the time. From the moment we wake up, we have an innate sense of our own energy levels. Sometimes we wake up lethargic, perhaps depleted of energy due to physical or mental exertion the day before or a restless night's sleep or even an illness. Other times we wake up refreshed and ready to start the day, full of energy and raring to go. Most of the time we are somewhere in-between.

If you have been physically active, you feel the energy that you raise as your body heats up, your heart rate quickens, and your breathing changes. Similarly, if you meditate, you can feel your energy levels balancing out and your breathing deepening as your mind clears. When you sleep, you lower your energy levels even more so that your body can rest and repair itself for the next day. Your personal energy shifts many, many times during the day depending on your activities and whether they are mental, emotional, spiritual, or physical. If you've sat an exam, even though you've been physically still for hours, you may feel exhausted afterwards. That's because you've been focusing your mental energy on the test, to get the best results. It will affect the rest of your being. Often our energy is raised or depleted in many different ways without intention. We tend to live very reactionary lives, which affects our energy levels and our ability to work with energy. For the witch, it is crucial that we work with energy differently.

Imagine that we work with our own personal energy with intention rather than simply reacting to situations. Instead of raising our heart rate and getting angry when someone cuts us off on the highway, we simply shrug and continue on with our driving. We don't need to expend energy on that reckless or careless driver; we can conserve our energy for the things that really matter in our lives. That person is already down the road and not a part of our life anymore in any shape or form, so let's just get on with it.

Perhaps the boss is chewing you out at work. Imagine what it would feel like to simply be a mirror reflecting back the energy that is being directed toward you. No, I don't mean shouting back; mirrors don't shout. Mirrors are very still, like a pool of water that only reflects when it is absolutely still. Imagine being still, being grounded, and not letting the energy of the other person affect your own. The boss finishes shouting, you nod and leave the room without getting bothered and then head on over to HR to let them know about this inappropriate and unprofessional behaviour on the part of your boss. If you're lucky, HR will do something about it. You then go home without being bothered by the day's events, feed your cat, and go out for dinner with your partner. You leave this energy alone. You don't take it in, you don't feed it after the event, and you work to keep your own energy clear.

It ain't easy. But it is achievable with practice.

As energy is fluid, we begin to understand what kinds of energy we are taking in, holding on to, and using in our everyday lives. Most of us want to have good energy: energy that keeps us clear and focused, that isn't laden with negative emotions. Energy is energy, and it is what we do with it that makes it good, bad, or indifferent. Energy can be layered with intention or emotion. What we must remind ourselves is that we don't have to take on someone else's negatively charged energy. We can go out into the local city park and connect with the clear energy of a tree or the blue sky or the shining sun or moon. We can connect to the energy of the Goddess or the God. We can connect with the energy of those who love us, friends and family who nurture and support us.

In Witchcraft traditions, a witch works with their own energy, usually combined with that of the natural world. In Hedge Witchcraft this is most certainly the case. We seek out places in the natural world where we feel good energy, energy we are in tune with and that can help us shift our own inherent energy into something more balanced and flowing. We learn how to take this energy in to support and sustain us, and we also learn how to give back energy in a reciprocal, sustainable relationship.

We can't just keep taking energy without giving back. Have you ever heard of energetic vampires: people that seem to suck the life out of you, people you interact with who leave you feeling down or out of sorts or tired? They may or may not be doing this intentionally, but this is something that we want to avoid in our own craft. We also know that we must give back for the blessings we have received. We don't want to become energetic vampires ourselves. And so when we work with energy, we know how to give back, for otherwise the energy will not be fluid and instead be held and carried and directed to one thing, depleting the energy in other areas, like a lake that runs dry if it isn't being fed by streams and rivers.

Find a place outside, if you can, where you feel the energy is good. Take some of that energy within you, perhaps using the roots and branches meditation I've discussed in other books. For a quick recap, envision your feet are like tree roots going down into the earth. Breathe down into the roots, extending them deep into the soil. When you feel secure and strong, breathe the energy of the earth up into your body, flowing through you and out through the top of your body, imagining branches and leaves growing out from all angles. Breathe the energy of the earth into your body for several moments, exhaling that energy to create a network of branches above you. When that is complete, draw in another deep breath from the earth, then exhale that breath out through your branches. Then breathe in the air from your leaves and branches and take that into yourself, moving it down through your body and exhaling into your roots. Breathe in the earth energy through your roots all the way up to your branches, exhale out through them, and then breathe in the air energy through your branches, down through your body all the way to exhale through your roots. Repeat as necessary until you feel your energy is strong, clear, and good. When you feel energised and relaxed, pull back in your roots and branches, give thanks to the earth and sky, and let your love for them flow out from you in reciprocation. You can place your hands on the earth and let the love flow into the earth, and then raise your hands to the sky with the same intention. Love is a wonderful energy.

Later on, find a way that you can show your appreciation more deeply—do a litter pick in that area, donate to an ecological cause, support a local wildlife foundation. For what you take, you give back in reciprocity.

Earth, Air, Fire, and Water Energy and Ourselves

We know that all around us is the energy of the elements. We use them in ritual and in spellcraft. We can harness these energies, and often we will have affiliation with a particular energy. For me, that's earth energy.

We will usually have a dominant energy that we use regularly, whether consciously or unconsciously. Often it is related to our astrological sign (I'm a Virgo, so definitely earth). There are positive and negative associations with a surplus of energy in any given element. For me, my natural abundance of earth energy means that I am usually grounded, dependable, rooted, physically strong, and like to create nourishing atmospheres. It also means that I am stubborn, sometimes implacable, and find rapid change difficult. Finding which element you attune with most in your life can help you better understand yourself and show you both your strengths and weaknesses.

You can use the other elements to balance out any elemental energy you have within yourself, such as allowing the transformative energy of fire to help you create a quick transformation in your life. You might use the energy of air to relieve stubborn habits, or water to show you how you can flow and change in the world. Ideally we aim to keep our own energies in balance through an acknowledgement of our dominant energy first. Then we can operate from a place of balance and harmony.

Energy and Magical Work

Knowing more about how energy works, as witches we can use energy in our magical practices. Sometimes it is even good to just practice raising energy in order to keep those "muscles" strong.

If you've ever read a book on Witchcraft, chances are that you have seen the "energy ball" exercise described; hopefully you've given it a go. This is where you push out your own personal energy to form a ball of energy between your hands. You can then shape this energy into other forms, change its colour, pass it on to other people experimenting with you, programme it with an intention, and then push it back into your body. Many energy workers, such as Reiki practitioners, understand this concept well.

In Hedge Witchcraft we have many different ways we can raise energy. We aren't limited to a single practice or tradition; we do what works for us. Below are some examples of how you can work with or raise energy. Try them out if you haven't tried them before or maybe even adapt and change to create something new.

Tense and Relax

This simple technique involves tensing certain muscles all over your body, raising energy through exertion. When you cannot build up any more energy, you relax all the muscles at once and push the energy out toward your desired goal through visualisation.

Breathing

There are lots of yogic breathing techniques that you can use to clear, balance, raise, or lower energy. Ancient yogis have created pranayama techniques, which are different types of rhythmic breathing practices that affect the mind and body.

Here is an example of alternate nostril breathing that can be found in yogic practices. Inhale slowly and fully through the left nostril, holding your right closed by placing your thumb against it. When ready to exhale, switch the nostrils so that you are now closing off your left nostril and exhaling through your right. After a full exhale, inhale through the right while closing the left, and then switch again to exhale through the left. Repeat for around five minutes if you can, while maintaining focus on the breath and finding a sense of calm.

Chanting

Everyone knows that witches chant under the full moon, right? Well, that's because it's a very good way to raise energy! Chanting anywhere, anytime can cause a change in consciousness as well as raise energy, which equals magic. You might repeat a simple chant, such as "This land she knows me, she calls my name. This land she knows me, she calls my soul."[30] You might work with mala beads or rock back and forth or simply sit still with your eyes closed and focus your mind on the land. Through the power of the voice, you are raising energy and connecting with the energy of the land itself. For me personally, the most powerful magic happens when I stop chanting and feel the stillness that follows the charged air after a few minutes of chanting.

Drumming, Clapping

Many shamanic practices know the power of the drum. If you've ever been near a real drum beating quickly, you will understand the power that it has over the human body. If you've ever been to a nightclub or a rave or a rock concert, you will understand the power of the beat and rhythm that flows through you. If you don't have a drum, you can clap, which produces both a rhythmic beat as well as raises physical energy through the motion of the clapping. You can start slowly, bending close to the ground or even sitting on the ground. Clap faster and faster, raising your hands as the beat increases, until you are clapping madly above your head. When the energy is at its peak, release it in accord with your magical intention.

Dance, Movement, Posture

If you are able to move, you can raise energy. Even seated or lying down, you can hold a posture such as a hand mudra (hand positions used in Buddhism to create changes in consciousness) or raise your hands to the sky. When seated you can rock back and forth, which creates a wonderful

30 This is part of a chant called "This Land" written by Samantha Marks of Magical Malas and excerpted here with permission. Find out more at Magical Malas, www.facebook.com/MagicalMalas (accessed February 21, 2024).

energy for trance work, or you can simply use it as soothing energy for your body, mind, and spirit. There's a reason parents rock their children to sleep.

If you are able, dancing is a great way to raise energy. Feel your own personal energy rising and let the energy of your location flow into you, such as working with the element of fire by dancing around a fire in your back garden, with the element of water by being on the seashore, on a hilltop for the element of air, or in a cave for the element of earth. There are established dance methods such as 5Rhythms, which is a wonderful ecstatic dance practice that can connect you to the elements and your own soul.[31] If you don't want to dance, you can simply sway or do other simple movements to connect to exterior energies. I like to have my hands flat, palms facing down to connect with earth, hands raised and fingers spread to connect with air, hands flowing in and out and upwards to connect with fire, and hands cupped before me to connect with water. Often I'll combine this with a chant to raise energy, such as "Earth my body, water my blood, air my breath, and fire my spirit," or simply attune my own personal energy with the four elements.[32]

Treading the Mill

This is a practice from traditional Witchcraft here in the British Isles. It involves walking around an object such as a stang, used as a focal point to travel between the worlds. The physical exertion raises energy, which can then be combined with drawing earth energy up through our feet or combined with the energy of the locale in general to then shift consciousness into the otherworld for hedge riding. It can also be used to raise energy for spellwork.

The Cone of Power

This is a technique often used in Wicca. It is traditionally performed by groups but can be done solo as well. Different groups will have different ways of doing this work. Some might stand in the circle and hold hands,

---

31 Roth, *Sweat Your Prayers.*
32 Visit my YouTube channel, Joanna van der Hoeven, for an example of this chant: https://youtu.be/4JuuYITWlyY (accessed March 21, 2023).

raising the energy within themselves and passing it along hand to hand. When the energy has risen to its height, the cue is given and the energy is directed up and out through a visualised cone to its target. Other groups might hold hands and dance around the circle to raise energy, and when the cue is given, they fall to the ground while pushing all the energy out. This energy is directed by the High Priestess or High Priest up and out through the cone and sent toward its target (or to manifest in the world). A solitary practitioner can do this on their own, but they will have to be both the energy raiser and the energy sender at the same time.

. . .

There are so many different ways you can raise energy. Some witches use sex to raise energy (either alone or with a consenting partner); others might feel their energy rising during thunderstorms and harness that energy alongside its elemental counterpart. You might imbibe a magical, intent-laden coffee in the morning to get your energy levels going or have a piece of dark chocolate. I advise against using narcotics or mind-altering drugs (herbal and chemical) to raise energy or create a change in consciousness because I believe we are much safer and healthier when we are in control. Taking some substances causes us to relinquish control, so the intention behind the work is also surrendered, which is not something I am willing to do personally.

Experiment with different ways to raise energy. It's only through experience that you will understand what works for you and what doesn't work. What doesn't work can often be our greatest teacher. Try some of these techniques before you cast a circle or perform a hedge riding or in your spellcraft. As well, use these techniques as an offering to give back some of your energy to the earth, and don't be afraid to dance your prayers.

Exercises

Try each of these energy-raising techniques and journal your results.

- Go out in nature and connect with different forms of energy. Approach with an open heart and respect. Ask permission before you go and hug that tree, for example.

- Meditate as much as you can to keep your own personal energies in balance.

- Find out what your dominant energy is and see if you can harness that energy in your work. As well, through journaling and meditation, see if you can find a way to balance out an overabundance of energy in a certain area.

I've been thinking too much again, trying to solve a problem that doesn't seem to have a solution. I'm driving myself crazy in the process too—well, crazier than usual.

I head outside and out onto the heath. I send a quick prayer to my Lady to help me find what it is that I need right now. The wind picks up; dark clouds approach. I stand and watch them coming toward me, wondering if I can make it home before the heavens open. I then remember my prayer for guidance and realise that this is just what I need right now.

The rain comes down gently at first and then it pours. There is no thunder or lightning, so I step out into the open and hold my arms out wide, taking in the rain, taking it into my body and my soul. I am drenched in seconds, but I don't care. The heaviness of the issue that was bothering me is gone, instantly flowing away down into the earth. I feel washed clean, soothed and soaking wet in the element of water. All around me there is the scent of rain.

My heart is eased, and I allow the element of water to show me the way through this difficulty. I realise that I am looking at the problem too analytically: I need an emotional response to this issue in order for the energy to flow. I thank my Lady for this insight, smiling and laughing as I spin around in the rain. As quickly as it came, the rain moves on, leaving a sparkling world of raindrops on tree branches, on the leaves, and all over the ground.

Drops of inspiration.

Chapter 6

Trance States

> I have dreamed in my life, dreams that have
> stayed with me ever after, and changed
> my ideas; they have gone through and
> through me, like wine through water,
> and altered the colour of my mind.
>
> . . . .
>
> Emily Brontë

Going into a trance state and riding the hedge is what defines us in our hedge riding practice. But just what exactly is a trance state, how can we get there, and what can we do once we're there?

Entering a trance state is so often misrepresented in our modern world. It seems like the definitions of a trance state have been made by those who have never experienced it. Here is how the online Collins Dictionary describes it:

> A trance is a state of mind in which someone seems to be asleep and
> to have no conscious control over their thoughts or actions, but in
> which they can see and hear things and respond to commands given
> by other people.[33]

We hedge witches, practitioners of magic, and walkers between the worlds know better, wherever we may be situated on this planet.

---

33 Collins Dictionary, www.collinsdictionary.com/dictionary/english/trance-state (accessed March 28, 2023).

Trance states are not always states in which you have no control, in which you have to surrender completely. Sure, there are instances where this work can be done, but the importance of hedge riding, for me at least, is to have the ability to have a foot in *both* worlds at the same time. That way, we can enter a trance state, still have the faculties to take note of what it is that we are seeing and doing, and come back to the mundane, agreed-upon reality with the knowledge intact. How else could we, as solo practitioners, do the work necessary and have something to show for it? We don't have people around us recording what we are saying, asking us questions, or taking us in and out of trance. We must do that for ourselves, and so a part of our body, mind, and soul must remain awake and aware in order to do so.

When I was in college, I took a course on hypnotism. One of the first things we learned was that hypnotism was certainly not what the media like to portray it as: a trance state where all control is given to the hypnotist. No, in hypnotism, just like in hedge riding, we have the ability to come "out of it" whenever we wish. We are not sublimating ourselves to another; we are not giving up our power and autonomy.

However, in some trance practices, this surrender is the whole point. Like being ridden in the Voudoun tradition, the practice requires relinquishing the self for the entity to enter and speak through you. In Hedge Witchcraft this too can be done, but remembering what happened during that state of surrender may be incredibly difficult, if not impossible, without outside help. We might record ourselves speaking in such a state and try to make sense of what is being said later on, but usually it just appears nonsensical without exterior questions and guidance by others.

Often in Wiccan traditions, a priestess will "draw down the moon," or aspect the Goddess, after which she can speak to others in the circle directly, much like being ridden by a Loa. The priestess sets aside her sense of self to allow deity to flow through, offering the deity's wisdom and advice to the coven as she deems fit. But hedge witches are solitary practitioners and therefore have no priest or priestess to do this work for them. They must be able to take themselves into and out of trance states themselves; therefore total control cannot be surrendered if one wishes to have any sort of memory or make sense of the event. A small part of the self must remain in order to say "okay, enough; time to come back," and it's that part that can also interpret the messages and experiences received.

We must work in both worlds at the same time whilst in a trance state. It's not actually as difficult at is may seem. In fact, I would say that it's probably easier to do than relinquish total control to another, even in divine form. It takes a lot of experience to be able to push the sense of self away and allow something else to come through you. It takes a lot of self-work and self-knowledge to be able to perform this sort of practice.

Another thing to remember is that trance states are not all that unusual. We humans, as well as some other animals, have an affinity for them. We can be entranced easily by things like a waterfall, a flame or fire, the clouds rolling above our heads, music and drumbeats. It's part of our nature to allow this sort of experience to happen.

We seem to be wired to accept trance states, while still being able to function. Think of driving your car and not remembering the last three miles you drove because you were thinking of something else. Your body was on autopilot; you didn't crash and were able to continue driving. While this is not ideal and you really should have been paying full attention to your driving, this highlights the fact that we can and do work in separate states of awareness all the time. We might wash the dishes and not actually think about the dishes. We might read a book and lose all sense of the outside world. What matters most is that we are in control of these trance states for the most part, and that we go into and come out of them at our own discretion. We pay attention to our lives and intentionally enter into trance states when we feel the need or desire. That is at the heart of hedge riding.

The brain operates using four different kinds of electrical brain waves known as alpha, beta, delta, and theta. (Science is still debating the validity of a fifth wave called gamma). Delta is the lowest at 0.5 to 4 Hz and occurs during sleep. This is when we are disassociated with the world, when we have "turned off" and gone to sleep. This is where we find healing, and so it is where young infants spend much of their time as they are developing so rapidly. We then have theta at 4–8 Hz, which is found in deep relaxation and inward-focused meditation. It's also the state we are in when we are under hypnosis. Next is alpha at 8–12 Hz, which is a relaxed, passive attentiveness that can act as a bridge between the external and internal worlds. Trance practices such as hedge riding often use a theta-alpha state (more on that below). We then have beta at 12–35 Hz, which is when we are active and externally focused and can range from a relaxed state to an anxious state. This is the state of the thinking self and ego-related issues.

Alpha-theta brain waves are being investigated for their potential to heal trauma and addiction. Doctors Nancy White and Leonard Richard looked at the work of Thom Hartmann (1997), whose commentary on it is fascinating to those of us who work and walk between the worlds.

> Everybody is familiar with the edge between normal waking consciousness and sleep: it's often a time of extraordinary feelings, sensations, and insights, particularly as we move from sleep into wakefulness . . . The Peniston alpha-theta protocol seems to enhance this ability to shift states, to move to this edge. In such states many aspects of the self involving wisdom and insight may be encountered and awareness of earlier traumas occurs, making them more accessible for healing.[34]

What we are doing when hedge riding and other trance practices is trying to reach that in-between state, that alpha-theta state mentioned above. This is where we encounter the otherworld, with all its wisdom and healing, adventure and challenges. It's telling that even these brain waves are neither one set nor the other but a combination of both alpha and theta. It's in those in-between places where the magic happens.

The hedge witch is usually always pretty open to what might be coming through from the otherworld when they are in a trance state such as a hedge riding or another form such as drumming, dancing, or other ecstatic trance practices. As hedge witches have a foot in both worlds most of the time, they often don't need much prompting in regard to trance practices

---

34 White et al., *Introduction to Quantitative EEG and Neurofeedback*, chapter 6.

to get where they need to go. Developing trance practices is extremely helpful to the beginner hedge witch, however, especially for those whom a trance state is not easily achieved. Once you are open and aware of the reality of more than just the so-called mundane world, you may not need to actively enter a trance state as much as you may have previously. You have already established a link and have a relationship with the otherworld and its denizens. With practice, you can shift your mindset with minimal effort to achieve your goals. The otherworld is right there on your doorstep, so to speak.

Practice different forms of trance states to find what suits you the most. Once you have gotten the hang of them, you may find that you require less and less time to enter into that trance state, and the effort to go in and out becomes much easier. You're working the muscle in your mind, in a manner of speaking, to train it to this new awareness. Once you have established a deeper connection with your *fylgja* (spirit helper), this becomes even easier. We'll take a deeper look at that in chapter 9.

I sit on the little bridge that spans the stream. The sunlight is dancing on the water, sparkling in an ever-shifting and changing flow. I feel myself quickly entranced here in this in-between spot that is neither on land nor water, on a bridge that spans not only this little stream but also this world and the otherworld. I open my heart to the otherworld, letting my rational Talking Self take a break. My eyes remain on the dancing motes of light in the water, and I am pulled into the otherworld. I ask, "What is it that I need to know right now?" I feel a slight nudge at my elbow and hear the sound of laughter tinkling by the water.

"You're not alone; you're never alone—and your shoe is untied."

I come quickly back to myself, but not before one of my shoes slips off my foot and starts to float downstream. Soon I am in the water, chasing after my shoe and laughing alongside Them.

Chapter 7

Magic

> We are jugglers with the vagaries of
> the universe. The important thing
> is to keep the balls in the air.
>
> • • • • • • •
>
> Vivianne Crowley, *The Natural Magician*

Here we are going to take a look at magic itself and the energies involved as well as a deeper look into the ethics of magical work as well as life in general, for it is all related.

But What Is Magic, Really?

Magic is often described as changing consciousness in accordance with will. When we change our consciousness, we also change ourselves. This is perhaps the most important part of magic. Magic is not about altering our environment and situation to suit our needs but rather changing the patterns of ourselves, the currents of energy that flow and weave in our lives that emanate from ourselves. When we change our consciousness, we are altering how we think and how we act. We are getting in touch with the energies of life that are more ethereal rather than tangible and shaping them by directing our consciousness through our will. This changes situations because it changes ourselves. There is a popular chant in Wiccan and Pagan traditions that goes: *She changes everything She touches and everything She touches changes.* This is magic.

Author Elen Hawke makes a very good point on magic:

> Magic is growth, for even when you use it for banishing or diminishing something, you are developing psychological, emotional and spiritual terms by the act of directing your own process.[35]

Magic not only changes external factors; more importantly, magic changes you. It sets the terms on which you will live and work.

Magic works on a deep, instinctive level. It works through symbols and imagery, feelings and emotions, as well as any physical paraphernalia that may contribute to the symbolism. Magic works through the Younger Self, that part of our psyche that works with symbols, images, and energy on a soul-deep level that Talking Self can't even begin to touch and can only think about as an abstract. Magic is visceral. It's where desire and fantasy come together through the direction of our will. Author Vivianne Crowley aptly describes it thus:

> When we enter the "grown up" world, most of us put magic aside. This is a pity because if we give up magic we forget that the mind can influence the body; that though accidental events can seem to dictate our lives, it is possible to have the right kind of accidents and to avoid the wrong kind. We forget that we have the power to influence how others react to us. We forget to be open to the strange patterns of events that can help us achieve our destiny. We forget the creative power of the human imagination.[36]

Magic is our birthright. It is something that is inherent in everyone, yet many people have forgotten how to access it within their souls. As children we often live magical lives, believing in things unseen, finding awe and wonder in the world. As "grown up" witches, we need to reinstate that magical sense of awe and wonder that we had as children, for that's where our magical power lies.

---

35 Hawke, *The Sacred Round*, 139.
36 Crowley, *The Natural Magician*, 1.

A teacher of mine (a völva) once looked deep into my soul while she was in trance and said to me: "Do you remember when you danced in the forest with the elves? Yes, I see you do. You do remember." Tears flowed down my face suddenly, as the weight of the modern world and all that I had gone through washed over me in a huge emotional tsunami. "Yes, I see that you have hurts, child. But remember the time when you danced with the elves in the wood. That is where your magic lies."

In our so-called civilised lives, we have forgotten how to access that magic. Work, commitments, chores, bills, surgery, etc. all take their toll on our Younger Self and on our magical lives that we so easily accessed when we were younger and freer from so much of the weight of the world. But as adults we can find that again, perhaps with an even greater notion of freedom, because we have an awareness of the preciousness of being in such a state of mind—free once more as we were when we were younger. With an awareness of Younger Self and magic, we can contact the unconscious to find out what it is that we need and what needs to be changed. We can speak to those parts of ourselves that the waking mind silences. We have the knowledge and experience of our years to guide and direct our magic while still working it with the joy and wonder of the Younger Self. We have responsibilities both mundane and magical, but the knowledge of these responsibilities does not restrict us; rather, it enlightens us toward a more intentional, wisdom-filled freedom, as opposed to a childlike, often ignorant view of the world. We must be adults and children at the same time; we must walk between both worlds with love and care.

Magic is not about imposing our will on the universe. Everything is connected. When we really come to understand that on a soul-deep level and not just on an academic level, then we begin to work our magic without letting ourselves get in the way. When we believe that we are disconnected from everything, that's where the ego is in control, and that is often where things start to go very wrong in our magic and in our lives.

Magic is about change, for sure, but that change is within as well as without. We cannot order the universe around to suit our whims and desires. Instead, we are working with the natural currents of energy to bring about what it is that we truly need in our lives. We must have a clarity of focus that is free from the ego in order to work truly effective, powerful magic. It also works in all aspects of our lives, and not just in relation to magic.

To live a magical life requires skill. This is a craft, after all. We must study, and we accompany that study with practice. This doesn't mean that we cast a spell every day, but we tune into the energies of the world around us and allow those energies to inspire us and help us live magical lives. When we watch the buds break open on the trees in the spring, we can be overcome with a sense of the beauty and magic in life that is unfolding all around us. We can tap into that energy, that beauty, because we are a part of it too.

When we begin to see our own self in the tree in the backyard, in the stars of the night sky, in the water that flows through our taps, we begin to understand the true connectivity that lies at the heart of magic. When we begin to identify Self with the world around us, then we are able to create change: change that is free from ego, change that benefits the world and is not just ego gratification. We learn to self-identify with the natural world around us, which changes us on a soul-deep level.

Growing Your Magical Abilities

Developing our magical abilities helps us become better in tune with the world around us. It's not about us seeking great personal power over the world; rather, it's about becoming more attuned to the wonder of magic that lies all around us, which ultimately leads to self-empowerment.

The best way to develop your magical abilities is to use them every day. Notice the magic that exists all around you. You can begin with recording your dreams, for in your dreams your deep magical self, your soul, is speaking to you. Pay attention to the natural world around you, even if you are in the heart of the city. Notice the sunlight, the wind, the birds, the insects, the phases of the moon. Take a moment each morning when you wake up to walk to your window or go outside, if possible, and take a measure of the day. A witch is one who observes, who pays attention. The endless energy of magic is all around you and within you all the time.

Deep in the heart of winter, when the snow lies five feet deep around you, there is the power of ice, water, stillness, silence, and sleep. Dancing around a roaring bonfire, there is the power of fire, of passion, of life's exuberance, of darkness and light. While drifting off to sleep, there is the power of liminality, of change and transformation, of healing and divination. While taking a bath or shower, there is the power of water all around you, attuning you with your emotions, gently guiding and holding, cleansing and changing you. Every act of life can be seen with a magical lens: it's all about perspective.

Author Starhawk puts it brilliantly in the seminal work *The Spiral Dance*:

> Magic is the craft of Witchcraft, and few things are at once so appealing, so frightening, and so misunderstood. To work magic is to weave the unseen forces into form; to soar beyond sight; to explore the unchartered dream realm of the hidden reality; to infuse life with color, motion, and strange scents that intoxicate; to leap beyond imagination into that space between the worlds where fantasy becomes real; to be at once animal and god. Magic is the craft of shaping, the craft of the wise, exhilarating and dangerous—the ultimate adventure.[37]

The craft of magic requires regular attention and practice, just like any other craft. It can bring us great joy, wonderful adventure, healing, and a closeness with the world around us on a thinking level as well as a deep intuitive level.

The Importance of Good Health

Being in good physical condition can really help us in our magical craft. This doesn't mean that you have to run marathons or be a certain size or weight, but rather that you are healthy. Eating well and exercising affects our bodies and our minds, so doing what you can to keep yourself in good condition will also boost your magical activities. Think of it this way: when working magic, you are manipulating energies, so it's a good idea to have

---

37 Starhawk, *The Spiral Dance*, 136.

the vessel that is working with these energies (i.e., you) to be strong. You wouldn't want to run many volts of electricity through old, weak wiring, would you? That's how buildings burn down. Instead, you want to ensure that you are doing all that you can to keep these energies going where they need to, carefully directed and effectively contained so that you and everyone else is safe. Eating whole foods, exercising, getting enough sleep, and eating sweets and drinking alcohol in moderation are good ideas when you are in the craft. Many witches, Pagans, Buddhists, and sects of Christian clergy are vegetarian. There is a reason for this: vegetarian diets, when done well, are usually very healthy. When we are healthy, it allows one to work with energies, such as working with the divine, in a more flowing, easy manner. Vegetarian diets are not for everyone, however, so talking to your doctor about the best diet for you, as well as a programme of exercise, is your best plan of action.

What else can we do to help develop our craft and make our spellcasting more effective?

Intention, Clarity, and Ethics

Our magic and spellcraft will be useless if we do not operate from a base of intention. We must know what it is that we need to change. We must be able to whittle that down to a very simple sentence or a handful of words. Honing in on the exact change is what will make your magic more effective.

We need to operate from a place of clarity. This means that knowing yourself, having an awareness of both light and shadow, is essential. Regular meditation, journaling, and doing soul work helps us achieve a clarity that will boost any spellwork that we do on any given day. If we are operating from a place of ignorance with regard to the self, we will lose that clarity and our magic will flounder.

We must also have a deep sense of personal ethics because we are part of the great web of life. Everything that we do affects us on a personal level in the physical, mental, and spiritual realms. It also affects others. We are all connected. It is that connection that allows magic to happen in the first place, so working from an ethical standpoint will make your magic stronger.

In many Wiccan and Witchcraft books you will come across an ethics section that details the threefold law, or the law of return. While I know there are many traditions in Witchcraft that do not follow this concept, some do, as well as most (if not all) Wiccans. The next part in this book that you are holding is a little different.

The Threefold Law

I don't think I've ever really believed in the threefold law in the way that most believe. In many, many sources, the threefold law states that whatever you do will return to you threefold. In a very simplistic sense, if you do good things, good things will happen, and if you do bad things, bad things will happen—times three. Many sources mistakenly state that this is a rule of karma.

I feel that this is a very odd Western misinterpretation of karma, for starters. Karma is not a system of reward and punishment. Karma is accepting responsibility for one's actions. It is cause and effect.

I feel that when we do magic or perform any sort of action, whether on the physical or metaphysical level, we affect energy. For me, this feels like a more appropriate definition of the threefold law. That energy is not only external to us but will affect us on three levels. Those levels are:

- physical
- mental/emotional
- spiritual

Let's take an example of cursing someone. If we curse someone, we must be pretty mad at them for something that they have done to us or someone else. That anger will have an effect on us at each of the three levels: physical, mental/emotional, and spiritual. We know that emotion, memory, and other things can get stored in the body, creating tension, stress, high heart rates, and more. As well, when we are angry, our mental and emotional levels change, and we become the anger if we are not careful. When we become the anger, we have lost our sense of self, our authentic, sovereign being, and allowed anger to take control. On a spiritual level, anger does not help us communicate with the world, the ancestors, spirits of place, deity, or anything on a deeper level. In fact, it can be a great hindrance to it, as integration is at the heart of most spirituality and religion. Anger separates us from everything else. In an earth-based tradition such as Witchcraft, where we believe that deity is immanent, this means that when we are angry and curse someone, we do not recognise the divinity within others. Our ego has one hundred percent taken over. We have separated ourselves from the world and created "the other." This "other" we can attack because we have chosen to view them as separate from the web of existence. In reality, everything is connected, so when we curse others, we are, in effect, cursing ourselves, the gods, everything.

We will all get angry. It's just a part of life. There is great injustice that requires anger for things to change. But how we use that anger is all-important.

The popular interpretation of the threefold law to me feels more like a reward/punishment system to keep people in line in an overly simplistic fashion. It states that what you do comes back to you three times—three times bad and three times good. It requires people not to think too much about all the areas in between the concepts of "good" and "bad," or even how those concepts are relative to each person and their own experience. It also doesn't acknowledge the deeper levels of meaning that can occur if we ponder this "rule" more closely. To me it just seems too close to a heaven/hell concept, which I find too simplistic to give much attention. Others may disagree, and I honour their perspective, but it just doesn't work for me.

So, looking more deeply at the threefold law, if we do something bad, like cursing someone, then it could be said that on a certain level it comes back to us threefold, but not in the sense that seems to be very popular, i.e., do good and good things happen, and vice versa. Rather, if our actions are not honourable and we do things to harm other people, we are in turn harming ourselves, our environment, our gods. Harming others causes suffering, both externally and internally, in a threefold pattern: we harm our physical, mental, and spiritual well-being. We've lost that connection to everything else—that sense of integration and integrity.

If we curse someone, we affect ourselves physically by holding on to that energy. That also affects us mentally, and if our curse does indeed work, it might even lead us down the road to more cursing. This leads to a reinforcement of such behaviour as well as reinforces the anger within us, which will make us physically and mentally suffer more and more. We may allow our egos to take full control; we might think we are better than others and that we have the right to punish as we please. We may even start going on the attack, full of ourselves and our power. On the flipside, we may fall into a deep depression by holding on to this anger and feeding it instead of seeing the positive in the world around us. We will become angry people who become depressed people. This all has an effect on us spiritually as well, for we have denied the existence of deity outside of ourselves. This severely limits our perspective of the world and continues an ever-increasing downward spiral of behaviour that causes suffering both within and without.

So, the threefold law can affect us in three different ways, but it's not as simplistic as some would have you believe. It's simple, yes, but not simplistic. Let's not get the two muddled!

And, if in doubt, you can always follow this great maxim: *Don't be a jerk.*

Like Attracts Like: The Law of Attraction

A lot of magic uses correspondences in order to achieve success, according to the principle of "like attracts like." This can also work in our daily lives, but it doesn't mean that doing good things will make good things happen to you, or vice versa. We can't control reactions to actions on that level. We can try using magic to persuade a favourable outcome, and when combined with a good ethical stance, this would be for the benefit of the whole. But there is a still a problem.

Many within Western Paganism have heard of the Hermetic principle called the law of attraction, especially if you have been working magic. However, I often see this oversimplified in books, stating that "if you put good energy out there, good energy will return" and vice versa. Not only is this trying to oversimplify the law of attraction, but it's actually incorrect as well, in my opinion. I know plenty of good people who have had bad things happen to them and some bad people who have had good things happen to them. I know, not all people are good or bad all the time, but it's just a thing: we live in a shared reality where we can't control the actions or behaviour of others, so sometimes, no matter what energy we are putting "out there," things will happen that will be contradictory to what we are attempting. As well, we are viewing the lives and situations of others from our own perspective and don't know everything that is going on outside of our own lives.

It's similar to the notion that posits "we create our world and our reality" that is so prevalent in New Age circles and in much of modern Paganism. To an extent this is certainly true, but then we have to realise that this is also a *shared* reality, so it will be influenced by other people's realities. As such, there is war, racism, sexism, etc., and people, no matter how lovely, compassionate, and beautiful, will fall prey to these circumstances despite what they are trying to create in their own world/reality. We can only control how we personally are in the world. We can attempt to influence others with our words, deeds, and actions, certainly, but not control.

There is, however, an aspect of this which is very significant and is the most important to work with, in my opinion. It's all about focus. What we choose to focus on can and will determine how we work with energy and what the resulting reality will be for us.

Say we stubbed our toe getting out of bed. Ouch. It's pretty bad, and we're limping around, swearing or just trying to breathe through the pain (or both). Finally we make it downstairs, and as we're taking the orange juice carton out of the fridge, we drop it and it goes all over the floor, giving us a nice sticky mess to deal with while we're already late for work. Then our train gets cancelled and we're over an hour late, and the battery in our phone is dead so we can't even call in. We get to work and tell everyone what a horrible day we're having, wondering what awful thing will happen next. You get the picture.

But what if we changed our focus? All the bad things that happened before work still happen. We get to work, but instead of telling everyone how we're having a really, really bad day, we just get on with it, turn our focus to our work and our colleagues, and at lunch go limp outside for a bit with our bruised toe and see the first daffodils of the season. In the previous example, I doubt one would notice the daffodils or even go outside if they were set on the theory that this day was, indeed, terrible. Things can snowball, depending on our perspective, and a lot of it has to do with our choice of reactions to things. Because we chose not to focus on the negative things that happened during the day, we were able to see the positive, the beautiful, and be inspired. We don't ignore the negative, but we choose what it is that we focus on. In choosing, we have personal sovereignty.

Because with situations like this, how we react is a choice. We can continue to focus on all the bad, negative things that have happened to us in our day or we can choose to focus on the daffodils, the colleague that helped us out, the boss that understood the trains were cancelled and said it was okay (she was late too), and so forth. Our focus is all-important. And when our focus shifts, we bring more perspective into our lives and notice more because of that shift in focus. So, in this regard, the law of attraction does indeed work.

Remember that, for the most part, what you focus on is your own choice. When really bad things happen and we cannot choose to settle our focus elsewhere, we just have to live through it, day by day, moment by moment. Eventually we will have the choice once again to move on or stay stuck. We cannot drown in the negativity when we have the option of choice. Use the law of attraction to your benefit and to the benefit of the world.

A Few Simple Spells

A chapter on magic wouldn't be complete without some spells that you can work, so here are a few simple and easy to do spells for the hedge witch.

A Charm for Protection

What you will need:

- a black or red pouch with drawstring or other way of sealing shut
- black pebbles or crystals: tourmaline, onyx, obsidian
- a mix of herbs: hydrangea petals, cloves, garlic, rosemary, oak leaves or bark, red geranium
- salt
- anything else that speaks to you personally of protection
- representations of the four elements
- an offering
- optional: a few strands of hair or nail clippings

Perform this spell during a waxing moon, if possible, or a full moon. If you work with a deity such as Andraste or Hecate, a dark moon also works well. Tuesday, Thursday, and Saturday are all good days to perform this spell. This spell can be worked indoors or out.

Gather everything together on a suitable work surface or your altar. Take the representations of the four elements and place them in their proper directions, such as a stone in the north, incense or a feather in the east, a candle or piece of lava rock in the south, and a bowl of water in the west (if those elements correspond to those directions in your landscape; if not, place them as appropriate). Ensure that any candles are safely placed on the work surface and away from you.

Call in the four elements using this or a similar chant:

Earth, air, fire, and water
Gather round and bless your daughter

Take a moment to ground and centre. Then, feeling the four elements around you, draw energy up from the earth, from the air around you, from the sun or candle's flame, and from the bowl of water. Hold these energies within you, mingling it with some of your own energy, and then place your hands over the items/spell ingredients. Now push that power out through your hands and into the items, infusing them with the elemental energy.

Then pick up the pouch and put the ingredients in, saying something like:

Hydrangea and geranium for my protection
Tourmaline and clove for my protection
Oak and rosemary for my protection
Salt and garlic for my protection

You may also place hair or nail clippings in at this point to seal this charm bag to you.

Invoke any deity that you work with, if any, and ask them to send their energy into the spell.

Tie up or seal the pouch, then hold it in your hands. Envision yourself shielded with a glowing ring or sphere of protection around you, or wearing a suit of armour or holding a magical, protective shield. Infuse this into the charm. When finished, say something like:

This charm is sealed for my protection
Safe from harm in any direction
By the powers of earth, air, water, and fire
This is my will and my desire
Protect me, protect me, protect me
Protect me, protect me, protect me
Protect me, protect me, protect me
By the power of three times three
This is my will; so mote it be

Thank any deities that you may have worked with and thank the elements for aiding you in your work. Leave an offering for them. Wear or carry the pouch on you at all times or hang it in your home, your car, or wherever you feel the need.

A Spell for Inspiration

What you will need:

- 1 cup, chalice, or goblet

- mead or water

- a stone from the land where you live

Get into a special place just before sunrise. This could be in your altar room by an open window, your back garden, in a wild place where you like to work, or even in a brand-new place (which can be even better for opening up new pathways). Face the direction of the rising sun, fill your goblet with your chosen liquid, and place it before you.

Create ritual space however you see fit. Stand or meditate with your eyes closed. Hold the stone in your hands and connect with its energy and the energy of the land around you. Focus on your intention: *to gain inspiration*.

When you feel the sun rising over the horizon (you'll need a sunny day for this, ideally), with your eyes still closed, feel it flooding over your body. Let the sun wash over every inch of your body, infusing you with its glorious golden light. When you are ready, slowly open your eyes (keep them cast down so you don't look directly into the sun). Place your stone gently on the ground.

Pick up the goblet and raise it up to the sun. Say the following or similar words:

Inspiration I seek

Inspiration I find

Here in my body

Here in my mind

Inspiration within me

Inspiration around me

Inspiration flow through me

So may it be

Feel the power of the sun flowing into the liquid as you say these words, then take three sips of the sun-infused liquid. Feel it entering your body and your soul. It fills you with its power and energy, full of inspiration. Enjoy this feeling and pick up the stone, infusing it with the power of these thoughts and emotions, with this inspiring energy. Thank the energies that have been with you today. When you need an extra boost of inspiration, pick up the stone and allow it to send some of that stored energy your way once again.

Following this ritual, pay attention to what the universe is telling you. Pay attention to your dreams, thoughts, and feelings. Meditate and journal your feelings. Open yourself up to possibility.

Let the inspiration flow.

The Rowan and Red Thread Charm

I love this little folk charm, which is super easy to do. It's a simple protection charm that is perfect to do at the beginning of the year.

What you will need:

- dried rowan berries
- red thread
- a needle

In your magical space, get the above items assembled. Thread the needle with the red thread, and then one by one pierce the rowan berries and thread them. You can do a berry for each of the thirteen moons, for example, and tie a knot before and after each berry to keep it in place as well as seal in your intention as you tie the knot. Or create a larger charm that looks similar to a rosary or prayer/mala beads. With each berry strung, say the following traditional charm:

Rowan berry and red thread
Bring all evil to its sped

Hang it up in the home, place it in your car, or even wear it as a protective amulet.

Release from the Past Spell

This is a spell to release you from people that you feel are holding you in the past. I got the idea for this spell from an episode of *Northern Exposure*. Maggie, on her thirtieth birthday, canoes up a river to camp, write letters to those who are keeping her in the past, and then sets them to float down the river where they will be received (in spirit). The spell below does not set letters adrift in a river because our rivers don't need any more stuff in them that shouldn't be there, but rather buries or burns them.

What you will need:

- Paper and pen (if burying the paper, try to find unbleached paper and vegetable ink)
- A fireproof container and matches (if burning)

Sit in a quiet spot, perhaps at your altar or somewhere out in nature where you will not be disturbed. With your paper and pen, begin to write a letter (or letters) to people whom you feel are holding you in the past. State the relationship that you had with them, the good and the bad, and state clearly why you think they are keeping you locked in the past.

At the end of the letter, state the following or something similar:

I now release you
As I am released
No longer in the past
But in the present at peace

Hold the letter, put it in an envelope if you desire, and sit with it for a moment. Gazing at the letter, draw up energy from the earth through the base of your spine. Add your own personal energy and push this into the letter, visualising yourself being released from the past. Chant "I am released" nine times, and end with "By the power of three times three, this is my will; so mote it be!" Bury the letter or set it alight and place it to burn safely in a fireproof container.

It is done.

A Salt Bowl Protection Spell

If ever you feel that your home, your person, or your space needs some protection, a simple salt bowl can do the trick. Salt is a great energy neutraliser that will reset any negative energy that is unwanted in the home or your personal space and keep going any good energy that you have intended to bring in or leave. It works with your intentions while maintaining its own inherent qualities.

I love using sea salt. For me, this little ingredient uses all four elements: the sea (water), which is evaporated (air) by the sun (fire) and crystallises (earth). It's a great ingredient to add to any protection charms, talismans, spells, or amulets.

How to Make a Salt Bowl

Use a bowl made of natural materials (i.e., anything but plastic). Please remember that a silver or silver-plated bowl will require a glass liner, otherwise the salt will corrode the metal. A porcelain or pottery bowl will work well, but it's your choice and preference that matters the most. I use small ceramic pin dishes found at secondhand and antique shops, which can be bought for as little as £1. Car boot sales, flea markets, charity shops—all these are great places to find little pottery bowls that can be used not only for salt protection bowls, but to hold ingredients of all kinds in your spellcrafting.

Wash the bowl well and bless it with your preferred method: incense, blowing your own breath over it to align it to you and bless it with your energy, leave it out under the sun or moon, etc. Get some good sea salt, which isn't that expensive from the local supermarket. If you're lucky, you may even find sea salt that is local to your area. If you absolutely cannot find sea salt, then ordinary table salt will work in a pinch.

Pour the sea salt into your projective hand (the hand that you write with) and draw up energy from the earth. Then pour that energy into the salt through your hand, mixing and blending a bit of your own energy with it. Once you feel the salt is fully charged with energy, then pour it from your hand into your bowl.

Placing both hands over the bowl, programme the salt with your intention. Visualise the salt drawing in any negative energies from your space or person and neutralising it. If you'd like, you can add a dark-coloured stone, such as a piece of dark flint, obsidian, or tourmaline, and place it on top of the salt in the bowl for an extra added boost. Power up the stone first, as you did with the salt, and place it with intention on the salt. You can also add some dried protective herbs, such as rosemary, geranium, or hydrangea petals. Again, charge them up before adding them to the bowl.

Once everything is in the bowl and charged with energy and intention, repeat this little charm or say something similar:

> Salt of the earth, of water, air, fire
> Grant me this, my desire
> Draw in negativity from this place
> And neutralise bad energy in this space
> Only energy attuned with my will
> Will cross threshold, doorway, and sill
> By the power of three times three
> This is my will; so mote it be
> (then chant "protect me" nine times)

Place the salt protection bowl where you feel it is most needed. You can create several of them or even one for each room in the house. I would recommend one by the front door, one in the main room of the house where people gather the most, and one by the bedside. You may need to change the salt as needed: if you feel negative energy starting to creep back in, it's time to renew the spell! Or you can simply change the bowls in tune with the moon's cycles, the seasons, or a certain day of the week, whichever works best for you.

May you be protected and blessed!

Exercises

- Study or review the Hermetic principles. The most famous text is *The Kybalion*. Knowledge of the Hermetic principles can provide a deeper insight into how magic actually works and how the energy of the universe can be worked with in your own spellcrafting. Or look around you in nature to see how everything affects other things. How does the ant affect the soil, the tree? How does the tree affect the air? How does the air affect you?

- Journal how you feel about the threefold law. Revisit this entry and expand on it in three, six, and twelve months' time.

- Try one of the spells listed above. Record the effects, if any. Review them and, if possible, try the spell again with a personal tweak or two to see if it works any better.

SUGGESTED READING

Book of Witchery: Spells, Charms, and Correspondences for Every Day of the Week by Ellen Dugan (Llewellyn, 2019)
With easy-to-understand instructions, Dugan's personality and charm shine through this work.

The British Book of Spells and Charms: A Compilation of Traditional Folk Magic by Graham King (Troy Books, 2016)
A treasure trove of British magic.

The Natural Magician: Practical Techniques for Empowerment by Vivianne Crowley (Penguin Group, 2003)
This is a great, practical, down-to-earth work that also has examples from the author's own experience.

The Outer Temple of Witchcraft: Circles, Spells and Rituals by Christopher Penczak (Llewellyn, 2013)
A detailed account of magic from a prolific and respected author.

Spells and How They Work by Janet and Stewart Farrar (Hale, 2010)
A seminal piece from two of the most influential witches of the modern age.

Thorsons Way of Natural Magic by Nigel Pennick (Thorsons, 2001)
A great look at magic from a non-Wiccan, traditional British Witch perspective.

Witch Crafting: A Spiritual Guide to Making Magic by Phyllis Curott (Broadway Books, 2001)
This book is a solid foundation for spells from one of the pioneers of Wicca and Witchcraft in the modern day.

I've been attacked online by someone I've never met but who works in the same circles as I do. They are spreading vicious, horrible lies about me, and there's nothing I can do about it. They are trying to destroy me and my career, everything that I have done. Other people are joining in, people I've never spoken to in my life, saying how they've had dealings with me and jumping on the bandwagon. It's distressing, and it makes one wonder how people can be so awful to each other with no provocation whatsoever.

What should I do? I eventually respond with a single post to allow my side to be heard and then leave it at that. The attacks and lies continue for a couple of weeks and then slowly die off as the attention spans turn to something else. The online world can be both a wonderful and a horrible place all at the same time. In these trying times, I seek the support of my friends and family, and they help me get through it by reminding me of who I am because they, of all people, actually do know me. I briefly daydream about retaliation, but it's just a passing fancy, an emotional release that is never acted upon.

Months later, I am told that the person who attacked me is very, very unwell. A year later, I find that they are unable to work and that their life has changed considerably for the worse. I breathe deeply and am reminded that what we do—everything that we do—affects us physically, mentally, and spiritually. I am thankful that I did not retaliate with unkindness, with vitriol and vengeance. It was bad enough to have to be on the receiving end of that horridness. To be the cause of it, to take energy like that into my being, is simply unthinkable.

I have had several stark reminders of how energy works in my time here on Earth. Each time I am reminded that I am part of a great web, and everything I do, as well as the actions of others, ripples across the web, affecting everything. I've never understood the need or desire to be mean to someone, to be a bully, to try and take someone down. I will never send those energies out, ever, because I will never take them into my soul. Wherever I am placed on this great web, I neither need nor want those energies to affect me, to ripple across my threads and those of others, to radiate out from my being. There is simply no need.

I pray to my Lady that all beings have peace and that we all move forward with a deep and profound knowing that we are all related.

Part 3

WISDOM

Going Deeper

Chapter 8

An Intimate Connection to Deity

Faith is a trust in a sacred reality. But trust has
to be earned; you don't just give it blindly.

· · · · · · ·

Phyllis Curott, *Book of Shadows*

In this chapter we will look at how one can establish a closer relationship
with deity. If you choose not to work with any deities in your craft, then
please feel free to move on to the next chapter. Some people find deep,
meaningful experiences working with deity, and others simply do not see
the need. The choice, as always, is yours.

I have been fascinated with deity my entire life. When I was a little girl,
one of my favourite books was all about Greek myths, and my favourite
people in it were the goddesses and heroines such as Artemis and Atalanta.
These were people I wanted to know: people who had similar interests to
me, people who I could look up to and take inspiration from in many different ways.

Growing up in a loosely Protestant household in Canada, we never
really talked about deity except when we went to church a couple times
a year or when we were taking the Lord's name in vain (often in Dutch
because it sounds better that way). I'd always felt that Mother Nature

should be important, that she should be recognised in some way, but she was something that was "made up" by our society. I envied the spiritual traditions of the First Nations people, who had goddesses and gods in the natural and spirit world that they could work with, talk to, and pray to. I read any books I could find about the local Mohawk and Algonquin tribes and their relationship to deity. I was thrilled to learn of their openly matrifocal ways and of their female spirits and deities.

In my teenage years, I came across the fantasy fiction of the Forgotten Realms series, and there I came across goddesses of magic, luck, poison, disease, love, the forest, etc. Oh, how I wished that there were such goddesses still around that I could choose to work with (well, not poison and disease, but to each their own). And then in my late teens I came across Wicca, having been introduced to the Goddess in a class that I took in college called Magic, Religion and Science. In that class we watched a trilogy of films from the National Film Board of Canada, all about Goddess religion and how it was still being practiced today, resurrected for the modern world.[38] I was hooked.

I've now been working with Pagan deities for over thirty years, in various traditions. I have always felt a calling to work with a particular deity at different points in my life, for they could offer me the knowledge and experience that I needed at that time, and I felt that I had something to offer in return. When I first began working in Witchcraft, it was simply the Goddess and the God that I worked with in my own practice. After a couple of years, I began wanting a more intimate relationship with a deity, someone with a name that I could call her (and him), attributes that were similar to mine, or ones I wished to emulate.

The first named goddess that I worked with was the Morrigan, for she spoke to my wounded twenty-something soul. I read up on all that I could find on her: her myths and stories, the artwork that portrayed her. I was spellbound by her strength and energy, her fierceness and her beauty. One day I went to my favourite spot, my "power spot," as I called it, and lay

---

38 Donna Read, "The Goddess Remembered," National Film Board of Canada, https://www.nfb.ca/film/goddess_remembered (accessed June 26, 2023).

down in the long grasses. I looked up at the blue sky and quietly said something like: "Morrigan, if you wish to work with me, I am here, waiting for you." A few moments later, I heard crashing through the grasses and wildflowers; sitting up, I saw a line of black horses all coming straight toward me. I knew the horses were there on the other side of the valley: they were the big draft horses that pulled the sleighs in the winter and enjoyed lovely summer and autumn seasons spent here in the valley. But when they came quickly walking toward me, strung out all in a row (horses will usually walk one behind the other, not side by side), my heart thudded in my chest. They came and stood all around me, these huge dark beasts, just looking at me sitting in the grass. I slowly stood up and touched their soft noses. They whuffed and nodded their heads, then resumed their normal behaviour, munching on the grass around me. I had my sign, and it was a doozy.

I worked with the Morrigan for several years. I still have an affinity for her, a special place in my heart as she was my first patron goddess. I then sought out a named male deity to work with, and Cernunnos immediately sprang to mind. Antlers, Lord of the Wildwood—yes, he was definitely the one for me.

Since those formative years, I have worked with other deities, devoting a year or several years to each, depending upon where my life took me in its wild and crazy journey. I have worked closely with Nemetona, Brighid, and a local Celtic goddess, Andraste, of whom little is known save for what has been recorded of her in relation to the warrior queen Boudica. I have also worked with Herne, who has a similar energy to Cernunnos but is more local and a bit closer to home in depth of feeling, as it were. My patron goddess is Freya.

By working more deeply with a goddess or god, I find that not only do I learn more (mythologically, historically, spiritually), but I also come out as a different person. As a pantheist, polytheist, and animist, I see divinity within everything, in different streams of energy and manifestation, with all having something similar at the core, something that is indescribable but enticing, exciting, life-giving, and death-affirming. I personally cannot imagine not working with a deity in any shape or form, for it is central to my practice, though I respect that others may not feel the same way.

Finding a Mythic Cycle that Works for You

Many find the standard mythic cycle of a solar god and an earth goddess works well for them in their practice. Others might develop a cycle that may be more in tune with their local landscape. For example, I combine a bit of both into my practice. I honour the solar tides and the lengthening days or nights and see the God reflected in that cycle. I have also created something new that works for myself and that I have shared with other people, who seem to respond well to the idea.

For me, I also honour the God in his dual aspect of the Green Man and Herne the Hunter. At the Spring Equinox, the Green Man returns to the land to bring back the growth in all the local flora after a long winter slumber. At the opposite point on the Wheel of the Year, the Autumn Equinox, the Green Man fades into the land and the Wild Hunt prepares to ride out from the otherworld. Between the Autumn Equinox and Samhain is a liminal time when the Green Man is fading. Similarly, between the Spring Equinox and Beltane, the Green Man is slowly awakening. At these times, Herne the Hunter is also either coming into his power, preparing for his rides across the night sky, or falling away from view as the tides turn. I know that Herne rides again when the constellation of Orion is in full view and travelling across the night sky (mid to late autumn here in England).

This is not a myth that comes down from any lore. It is something that speaks to my soul, that makes sense to me where I live in the world. It also resonates with others in the local area. As such, I'm going with it because it works for me. It doesn't have to be ancient to be valid.

You might find another mythic cycle that explains the turning of the seasons that works for you, and that is brilliant. Go with it. Research as much as you can about the gods in your local area, should you wish to work with them, then go out and try to meet them. See what they have to say to you personally, which may or may not entirely correlate with what you have already discovered. The gods will tell you how they wish to be honoured.

How to Choose a Deity to Work With

Do we choose to work with a deity or do they choose us? Well, a bit of both, in my opinion. We may feel drawn to certain deities because they have qualities that we desire or admire. We might learn their myths and say a big yes to everything that concerns them. We might research local deities from the land where we live and want to work them more intimately (without culturally appropriating them). There are many different reasons why we would choose to work with a deity, but what about a deity that chooses us?

This can and certainly does happen. In a dark moon meditation, Andraste asked me if I wanted to be her priestess. Her voice, low and measured, filled a corner of my mind and offered me something new, something mysterious and rewarding. I said I'd think about it and subsequently turned it down. Several years later I worked again with her and still honour her as the energy and goddess of the land where I live. But I am not her priestess.

This is important: just because a deity calls out to you, it doesn't mean that you have to accept and work as their priest, priestess, dedicant, acolyte, etc. At the very least, you can think about it before you make up your mind and then politely accept or decline as you so choose. Some deities will change your life for the better and sometimes for worse. I have heard stories of people who have worked with Odin, for instance, whose lives were turned upside down much as he hung upside down on the world tree for nine days and nine nights. Many people who work with Hekate find that things swiftly begin to change as her energy weaves its way through their lives and lights up the dark recesses of the soul. Sometimes we are just not ready to work with a particular deity at a particular time in our life, and that's perfectly fine. We can only do what we can.

If we want to work with a deity and one hasn't yet called to us, how do we go about choosing? First, I would assess your lifestyle and temperament. If you feel called to the healing arts, then researching deities who have a patronage in that area of expertise is probably your first port of call. Then look to your ancestry, for you may find a connection or a calling there (though this is absolutely not necessary). Finally, do your homework and learn all that you can before you begin to work with a deity. Reading a single web page or coming across a definition of a deity listed in a witchy book is not enough; you must do the work. Why? Because when you work with a deity, you will be taking their energy into yourself, working with it and letting it influence your life. You want to make sure that the energy is right for you as well as think about the repercussions. Learning the deity's myths will certainly give you a good idea on that front, but you can also talk to people who work with these deities. How do these people seem? You may only be able to do this online, but you can still get a basic idea of these folks. Do they seem happy, well-adjusted, and healthy or are their lives a complete shambles from start to finish? It may or may not have something to do with the divine energy that they are working with in their practice. If so, consider your choice wisely.

If you do decide to go ahead and work with a deity, you can always do so on a trial basis. You don't have to commit yourself for life. Indeed, setting a time limit on your work with a new deity can be a good thing. Much like the coven tradition of a year and a day, you can use this for getting to know your new patron deity. I have certainly done so, and each year you can renew your commitment or walk away as necessary, with all due respect. You could try it for a moontide or three moontides (or a season) and see where it takes you, and if you're happy with that choice.

One last thing on this matter: don't forget that just because we have chosen a particular deity, it doesn't mean that the deity necessarily wants or is willing to work with you at that point in time. A trial period is a great way for both of you to get to know each other a little better and see if your energies work well together. At the end of this trial period, you both will know.

Deepening the Relationship

When you work with a named deity or the overall energy of deity, there are ways you can deepen that relationship. Prayer is usually the first port of call. Many who come from a background based in the Abrahamic faiths find prayer in a Pagan tradition to be odd at best and downright wrong at worst. But prayer is simply communicating with deity; it is not beholden to a particular faith. Our Pagan ancestors certainly prayed to their deities, and many in Pagan traditions still do today, for prayer is simply opening up the conversation with deity. There are many different ways to go about it.

Some like to do formal prayer with rehearsed lines, invoking deity into their lives. These prayers might be self-written or come from different traditions, passed down through the lore. Others prefer an improvised, conversational form of prayer, where one simply has a chat with deity. Some do both; I certainly do. It may just depend on what you are doing at the time. In ritual, you may perform both formal prayer (in the form of invocations) and informal prayer, telling the gods what you are thankful for or asking them for aid or guidance. What is important is that the line of communication is open.

When this line of communication is open, we are also open to the experience of awe. Awe is something that I most often correlate to deity; however, for those who do not believe in or have no interest in deity, awe can be seen in the natural world without a religious or spiritual overlay. As an animist and pantheist, I see deity in everything and am often overcome with feelings of awe in my interaction with deity in the natural world. This experience of awe helps me see the beauty in the world rather than focus on the negative and often depressing aspects of our modern-day society. By opening a line of communication with deity in this fashion, the experience of awe keeps me on an even keel.

In her study and experience of Witchcraft in the BBC Sounds podcast series *Witch*, India Rakusen learns about what awe does to our bodies, our minds, and our spirit.

> Awe has these measurable physiological effects on the body. So, in comparison with other positive emotions, it was only the emotion of awe which seemed to reduce levels of cytokines (which are associated with immune and inflammation response), which suggests that awe is, simply, really good for our health.[39]

---

39 Rakusen, *Witch*.

This is really interesting, as so many kinds of ailments are caused by problems with our immune systems. She goes on to add:

> Awe also seemed to affect the area of the brain called the default mode network, which is associated with sense of self . . . you have this sense of transcendence, and that is relaxing in some way . . . Awe makes people kinder and more generous.[40]

Getting outside of one's self by getting out of your own way and simply experiencing deity can bring about these feelings of awe, which leads to relaxation from the transcendent experience one usually feels in such a situation. For myself, it is also deeply inspiring and helps me get on with my day and my work in a new light, having been boosted by this experience. Watching a gorgeous sunset, communicating with the goddess Freya as a falcon flies past me on the heath, feeling the power of the North Sea as I stand on the shore at sunrise—all these lead to feelings of awe, which simply make my day and my life better.

I have always had experiences of awe in my life, from as far back as I can remember. It can be from something as simple as a tiny waterfall only a handspan high to watching an electrical storm rage over the sea. One of my favourite early memories is of a crab apple tree in the elementary schoolyard. I remember waiting for the bus and looking at the beautiful little red apples in the dappled September sunshine. I felt at peace with the world, and everything fell into place. I still recall this memory when I need that feeling in my life, where for that moment everything was okay, there were no demands or intrusions on my life; I was utterly and fully connected to nature, the tree, the sunshine, the earth, and the people around me. Another memory is of watching the sunset over a lake in Mont Tremblant Provincial Park in Quebec, Canada. The mist was beginning to form on the still water, the sun was just touching the horizon, and all around were the smell of the campfires. Suddenly the sound of bagpipes came floating across the water, as if the sun and lake themselves were making this music. I could feel my heart space expanding; for a brief glimpse in time, I knew

---

40 Rakusen, *Witch.*

the order of the universe. Even as I sit here typing these memories to share with you, a smile has spread across my otherwise harried face, as I have spent most of this busy day trying to accomplish as many things as possible in an attempt to catch up with work. I can feel my pulse has slowed and my shoulders have relaxed, and I know that everything will be accomplished in its own time.

Awe is most definitely good for you.

Once this line of communication is open, it is important to nourish the relationship and keep it open. It's not enough to just talk to this deity once in a blue moon (literally or metaphorically), but do so as you would do with a close relative or a cherished friend. Do not call on deity only when you want something; no one likes that, deity included. It would be like calling on a friend only when you want something from them, and this is the quickest way to end a friendship. Instead, talk to deity, share your appreciation for them, honour and pray to them daily. Prayer is not always a petition for something but can simply be a recognition of their presence in your life or a show of gratitude. Prayer can take on many forms, and it is up to you to discover them all in your relationship with deity.

Offerings are a great way to bolster your relationship. Give thanks with words, song, poetry, or material offerings in return for the closeness, the gifts, the blessings, and the feelings of awe that you have experienced. A good relationship with any being is a two-way street. You must give back, reciprocate for what you have received. Otherwise you will fall into the trap of taking and taking, which is the pitfall of modern-day society. Your relationship with deity is not a form of consumerism. Reciprocity is key.

I leave offerings of food and drink at each full moon and for each sabbat. On Fridays I leave an offering to Lady Freya. I also leave offerings for the things that I have accomplished, thanks to the inspiration gained from deity and the natural world. I pray almost daily to my deities, the land where I live, and all that share this space with me in this moment in time. I give my gratitude to the land (which can be viewed as deity) for the food that I eat and for the rain that falls in a dry season. I give my thanks to various deities for the gifts in my life and for the blessings of family and friends. All these acts help me reinforce that relationship to deity.

Deepening your relationship to deity is not something you can just read about. It is something that you must do. It requires effort, and the rewards you will see for yourself if you take the time and effort to do so in a consistent manner.

Suggested Reading

The Inner Mysteries: Progressive Witchcraft and Connection with the Divine by Janet Farrar and Gavin Bone (Acorn Guild Press, 2012)
A wonderful guide demonstrating working with the sacred and the divine.

Philosophy of Wicca by Amber Laine Fisher (ECW Press, 2002)
A really good look behind many principles of working with deity in Wiccan practice.

It is just after dawn at the Spring Equinox. A friend and I have gathered on the shingle beach, the North Sea stretching out before us in a vast expanse of grey, rolling water. The tide is at its highest, and behind us a lagoon has formed. We have finished our ritual and are now relaxing in the cold wind that blows over the water, wrapped up in winter coats, hats, gloves, and boots. It's always cold on the beach for this sabbat, but we don't mind. We ended our ritual with a prayer for our friend who had gone into labour the night before. We haven't heard anything, and so naturally we were worried for her. We prayed that everything would be all right and took this final moment to sit for a while by the lagoon on our way back to the car. My friend wandered around taking photos, and I sat near the water's edge, the calm, still water of the lagoon reflecting the colour of dawn. I thought about my friend and suddenly a grey head popped out of the water.

A seal swam there, three feet in front of me. It looked at me as if it had a message. "Hello," I said softly. My friend gave a small squeal of delight as she saw what was happening and proceeded to snap some photos. I looked into the seal's eyes and knew the message that it communicated from the Goddess. We spent around a minute just looking at each other and being truly present in the moment before it disappeared beneath the water and was gone, out to sea again.

"I think the baby has been born," I said to my friend.

"I think so too," she replied.

Huge smiles were plastered all over our faces as we drove home and left messages of congratulations. A daughter had indeed been born, and a new family had just begun.

Chapter 9

Working with Your Familiar

A black cat crossing your path signifies
that the animal is going somewhere.

. . . .

Groucho Marx

At some point in the working of the craft, you will come across the concept of the witch's familiar. Just what exactly a familiar is depends on the witch. Some witches see familiars in animal form, others as one of the Good Folk or Fair Folk (faeries). There are also plant familiars and stone/crystal familiars for those who work closely with these realms. Some view the familiar as a spirit that is bound to do the witch's bidding (almost like a form of spiritual slavery, in my opinion, and that's never good). Sometimes the familiar, especially in traditional craft practices, is seen as an extension of the witch's own spirit or soul in the form of a fetch. Others may see the familiar as a thoughtform that one creates to perform a specific task, such as to carry out investigative work or a spell.

Then there are also helpful spirits that may fall into the category of a familiar spirit, such as a household brownie or the obliging Red Goblin, as seen in *Aradia,* Charles Leland's seminal work on Witchcraft. There is also the Scottish Wag at the Wa', a fireplace spirit that helps with cooking, or even the Hobbitrot or Habetrot who helps with spinning, weaving, and textile work. The Hobbitrot may have its roots in Germanic lore, meaning "Red Hobbit" (similar to Leland's Red Goblin) and which I believe may have influenced J. R. R. Tolkien in his work.

The Animal Familiar

The most popular image of the witch's familiar is the traditional black cat, followed by a toad or a newt. There are medieval woodcuts with witches sharing the names of their familiars, and those names are popular again today for modern-day witch's pets/familiars. Maybe you have heard of Pyewacket, Griezzell Greedigutt, or Vinegar Tom. I know at least two people who have Pyewacket as a name for their familiars.

Animal familiars in Traditional Witchcraft are those that have been raised by the witch themselves, purportedly fed small amounts of blood to deepen the bond between them, and also should share the same bed when sleeping and dreaming, to create a close relationship.[41] Once the bond is secure, the witch can then charm the animal into doing their bidding, such as spying, theft, or other nuisances. More positive work has not been documented, but I am sure that there are instances where this may be the case.

Outside of Traditional Witchcraft, familiars take on a slightly different role. Rather than doing the witch's bidding and foregoing the feeding of blood (because, well, *yuck*), the familiar is more of a helping hand in a witch's work and daily life. They are more likely to choose their person (cats don't have owners; they have staff) and willingly give of their own time and energy to help with whatever it is that the witch is currently doing in their craft. The familiar will sit with the witch during ritual and especially during any magical work. They will often lean up against you to send you some of their own energy to help boost the work. They also know when you are low in energy, when you may be under some sort of psychic attack, or stay close to you when you are physically ill. They may enter your dreams so that you may see through their own eyes, much like the Traditional Witchcraft familiar (though this is a voluntary thing, shared by the

41 Pearson, *Practical Craft Working*, 175–176.

familiar of their own free will). You won't need to have raised the animal from birth, and one may come to you at any time in your life. The most common is, of course, the cat, but dogs and rats are also popular today.

Let your animal familiar come to you. Seeking one out will usually not yield results. You may have a predetermined idea of the animal that you wish to work with, when really what you may require is something completely different. Therefore, it is best to allow the animal to come to you and make itself known. Pay attention to any contact you may have with animals in your local area. This could even be unconventional, such as a magpie that has decided to befriend you. You may even have more than one familiar if it is deemed necessary for your work. Honour the animal(s) in a respectful way; take good care of them at all times. It may be a household pet or a wild animal, so treat it appropriately. Take all due precaution and care with wild animals, for they may act in ways that you won't understand and could be dangerous. Always be sensible, first and foremost. For example, I was working closely with a deer familiar (see below) but still needed to be cautious around them, especially during the rutting season. Stags can cause great harm, so common sense is vital when working with and encountering any wild animal.

Sometimes a familiar spirit from the otherworld may take on the shape of an animal. This may be an animal that keeps appearing in your life and may be of an unusual size, shape, or colour. This is often referred to as a *fylgja*, from Northern European Paganism. For years when I was deep diving into my hedge riding practice as well as working with the goddess Freya, a white doe kept appearing on the heath where I live, watching me from a short distance. I felt like she was guiding me on my journey and sharing messages with me from the otherworld. One look into her eyes and I was immediately between the worlds.

The fylgja is a spirit companion that has been with you since birth but takes on an animal form in your lifetime in order to share information, guide, or guard you. It is probably most often seen as a guardian spirit, and the term *fylgja* stems from Scandinavian lore. Not only can the fylgja travel between the worlds with you, it can also share messages from the otherworld and deity.

The Faery Familiar

Many witches throughout history have worked with the Fair Folk, or the faeries. As demonstrated in the first chapter of this book, we have very old accounts of accused witches working with the faeries or deriving their power from them, which in some places wasn't considered as bad as consorting with the devil (though later they became one and the same). Remnants of old faery practices may have survived down the long line of history and are being investigated and re-created today for the modern witch. The hedge witch knows that there is great benefit to having a faery familiar, a guiding spirit from the otherworld who can help you navigate the complex realms beyond this world.

A faery familiar is usually not a small cuddly fluttering butterfly-winged lady. Though they can take on many different forms and come from many different tribes, this Victorian fantasy has been perpetuated into the modern day. Now, I won't say that faeries will *never* appear like this because you can't put an absolute on the Fair Folk. However, in traditional folklore the faeries are a power that needs to be approached with caution and respect.

Here in the UK, the most common tribes of Fair Folk are the Germanic light and dark elves, the Irish sidhe, the Welsh tylwyth teg, and the Scottish seelie courts. There are many, many other kinds of faeries, but to go into detail would require an entire book in itself!

The fairy familiar will be a useful guide in your hedge riding experiences to the otherworld. They may also help you in your herbcraft, spellcraft, and finding places of power. They are a very important ally to the hedge witch and should be treated with respect. To have a fairy familiar is a traditional and very rewarding experience.

Plant and Other Natural Familiars

Some witches, especially those who work with the plant realm, often have a plant familiar. This is a type of plant that they often work closely with and with whom they are deeply attuned. It might be an herb, a type of flower found in the garden, a bush, a shrub, or a tree. When I was young, I had a birch tree familiar whom I spoke to regularly and who helped me with various troubles. This particular tree lent beautiful, inspiring, and calming energy and was a vital part of my growing up. We would exchange energy, tales, and wisdom, and I will never forget her.

When looking to obtain a plant familiar, see which plants growing in your area make you feel at home. Find out which ones want to "talk" to you and share their energy with you. You will know it when you feel it. As with an animal familiar, take good care of your plant familiar and it will take good care of you.

Stones can often act in similar ways to plant familiars. If a particular stone attracts you, try to commune with it. Some may want to lend you their energy and are openly willing to work with you straightaway. Others may need to be coaxed through establishing a respectful and reciprocal relationship first and foremost.

Water can sometimes work as a familiar spirit too. The energy of a river, a stream, or a waterfall can help you in your work and your hedge riding experiences. It can lend you its energy and enjoy yours in return in harmonious, balanced reciprocity.

Everything in nature has its own energy and spirit. Animism is integral to the hedge witch's worldview. We are all just energy and spirit made manifest. When a soul calls out to you and opens their soul to yours, whether it is of a stone or a plant, a cat or a dog, you will know. It's a deep honour and one that should be treated with great respect.

The Fetch Familiar

In Traditional Witchcraft, the body and soul are seen as having three aspects: the physical body, the soul/spirit, and the fetch.

The fetch is sometimes seen as the opposite sex to the practitioner, much like the animus or anima of Jungian psychology. Then again, they may be of no gender at all. Sometimes the fetch may be seen as the otherworldly spiritual partner to the witch. Others see it as a type of female guardian spirit that walks and works with the witch during their lifetime. This may be the origin of the fairy godmother. The fetch can also assume animal form and may be confused with the animal familiar. The difference is that the fetch is a part of the witch's personal earthly matrix, whereas the animal familiar is external to the witch.

As the fetch is a part of you, it is up to you to discover it. You could perform a hedge riding to contact the fetch aspect of yourself and establish a relationship with it. When you have need, if there is a good relationship between you, the fetch may help you in your work. The fetch will help you deeply understand your own self and may bring disparate parts of your being back together. You may get in touch with parts of yourself you never knew you had. You might also send your fetch out to do certain work for you, depending on your need. Working with your fetch can be a deeply transformative experience.

To contact your fetch, perform a hedge riding while in a cast circle or hallowed compass. Ensure that you have an offering for them with you that you can give to them on the physical plane. Call to them in your own words and speak honestly about your desire to contact them and learn more about them. Stating your desire in a prosaic way three times, with full intention and emotion behind the words, can often call your fetch's attention to your work. After that, it is up to you to keep that relationship going, ensuring that your awareness of your fetch is with you at all times.

The Thoughtform Familiar

This type of familiar is found again in Traditional crafting. It is sometimes called a servitor. A thoughtform or being is created by the witch and housed in a particular natural object, such as a stone. In a way, you are bringing this being to life, to manifest here on this earthly realm. Your emotions and personal energy create the thoughtform so that they can aid you in the manifestation of your spellcrafting. They aid you in your work and have a deep connection to you through your own energy. You may set a certain time limit on this being's existence; always ensure that it will travel with you or return to the energy fields from whence it came upon your death. You may desire to work with this creation for a year or maybe even a day. It will largely depend on your need.

You may create a thoughtform and send it into a stone. This stone then resides in or on the property, as per the need. Some witches may put the thoughtform into an amulet they can carry with them at all times. You will need some sort of natural object to house the thoughtform; be careful with it. Should the housing break, the thoughtform's energy may run rampant and some clean-up duty will be required. Similarly, losing the housing will require careful work in summoning the thoughtform back to you. Remember, you are working with energy here, so you need to ensure that it is done carefully and with respect.

Here is an example of creating a thoughtform familiar. Say you require protection for your home from physical and astral entities. You may find a large stone in your local environment that wishes to work with you. Great! Ask this stone whether it can house a thoughtform for you and lend its energies to your work. If the permission is given, then, in a ritual space, hold the stone to your forehead, heart, or solar plexus region and summon the need from deep within. Visualise a form for this need, such as a guardian in plate armour that wards the entrances to your home who can turn away all unwanted physical and psychic energy. This thoughtform is created from your energy and is tied to you and your intention. Push this thoughtform into the stone and welcome it to its home. State the intention for the thoughtform out loud three times. Then state the duration that you require for the thoughtform's existence; it could be for a year or a lifetime. Either way, when the duration is up, ensure that you say the appropriate wording to either take the thoughtform with you when you travel into the lands of the dead or that it dissipates accordingly back into the world's energy matrix with harm to none. Don't forget that if you have put a specific time limit other than your lifetime, you may need to create a new limit if you wish to extend it for any reason before the designated time is up.

Give offerings regularly to your created thoughtform. Remember that it is not your slave but a form of energy that you have created to help you in your craft. As such, it requires respect, sustenance, and reciprocity. Talk to it daily, say hello, wish it well, thank it for its help in your life. Give offerings such as water, milk, incense, or whatever you think it would like. Don't neglect it; rather, treat it as a friend and ally in your life.

Exercise

Have a go at communicating with and establishing a relationship with each kind of familiar in your practice. Take your time with this; you don't have to do it all in one day or even one month! As well, try creating a thoughtform familiar: a good suggestion would be to create one to protect your home. In chapter 14 there will be a detailed ritual to create your own thoughtform familiar for this very purpose.

I kneel on a cushion before my indoor altar. The candles are lit and soft music is playing in the background to cover up the noise of the television downstairs. An oil burner is letting out an enticing and rich scent. The scene is set to create a little magic.

I am doing a healing spell. I have apple twigs for health, oak bark for strength, and borage for courage all contained in a little saucer. The herbs have been charged. I pick up a jar candle and write symbols on it with a marker pen, then anoint the top of the wax with sandalwood oil. I place the candle in the middle of the herbs in the saucer that is sitting atop my pentacle and prepare to send energy into it.

The door that was pushed shut but not fully closed is suddenly opened a few inches, and my familiar, my cat, comes in. He takes one look at what I'm up to and plops himself against my leg. I can feel him sending me energy for the spell, and I thank him silently with a pat. I draw up energy from the earth, from my own being, and mingle that with the energy that he is giving me. I send it into the candle, holding my hands on either side and programming it with my intention, visualising the person being healed, happy, healthy, and whole. As I pour more energy into the candle, I say a charm, repeating it over and over again. When enough energy for the work has been sent, I stop the flow and shake off my hands. I sit quietly for a moment to regain balance, and then I pick up the matchbox and strike a match. "So mote it be," I say as I light the candle wick. I can feel the energy bursting from the flame out into the world, going to its target. I say a prayer to the deities, and the work is done.

I sit with the candle for a while, my cat still with me. It is now time for bed, so I carry the lit candle surrounded with herbs on the saucer downstairs to the now empty and dark living room. There I place the candle and saucer safely in the fireplace to burn throughout the night and for the next few days. I will repeat the charm and visualisation in the morning and again before I go to bed. I will do this every day for seven days until the candle burns out completely.

My familiar follows me every step of the way, sitting with me as I place the candle in the fireplace. I can feel him sending me some extra energy to replenish my own. I thank him, and then we both head upstairs to bed.

He's such a good boy.

Chapter 10

Your Own Herbal Allies and Practice

Every hour spent in front of a TV screen shortens your life by 21 minutes, whereas every hour spent gardening lengthens it.

. . . . . .

Gardener's World Magazine, Feb. 2018

In my previous book, I offered eight hedgerow herbs that can be used in the craft of the hedge witch. In this chapter, we will look at more herbs for the hedge witch, as well as different methods of using the herbs in your own craft.

Finding your herbal allies can be a greatly rewarding part of your craft. I believe that all hedge witches should have at least some knowledge of the plants that grow in their area. The beings of the plant kingdom are no less important than the other beings we share our existence with. In fact, were it not for plants, we wouldn't exist at all. The fact that we have oxygen to breathe is all thanks to the abundance of plants that live on this third rock from the sun. We live in a symbiotic relationship with plants, as they provide the oxygen we need to breathe, and we provide them with the carbon dioxide that they need to breathe. We are all part of a functioning ecosystem, where each has its own part to play. Understanding our role and finding allies in our work helps us grow in our own personal power and in our craft.

It's important to work first and foremost with the plants in your area. Why? Well, these are the plants that you can observe in all seasons and really get to know intimately. When you watch a patch of nettles suddenly sprout from the bare earth in the early spring and keep a watchful eye on them, knowing when is the perfect time to harvest some for your tea or for a nettle soup, you will have truly connected with the plant through careful study and observation. But don't forget that this is a reciprocal relationship; you are not just an observer. Offering something back for what you receive is vital in order to establish a good relationship with your herbal allies. Fresh, clear water is always appreciated, as is food that they enjoy, such as a natural fertiliser. Sitting with a plant and watching it grow day after day is a wonderful way to connect to the plant realm. You can even speak to the spirit of the plant; be assured that it will respond. It's been scientifically proven that plants respond to sound, and sound is vibration.[42] Plants, like us, respond well to good vibes!

It's a good idea to keep a plant journal. In it, record the different plants that you wish to work with in your area. Note the time of year that they sprout, flower, seed, and die back (if they do). Try to draw the plant: even if your artistic skills are very basic, drawing something makes you pay close attention to the object you are drawing, and you will notice the small details that may have previously eluded you. Take photos from all different angles, print them out, and paste them in your journal if you don't have the time for drawing. Talk to the plant, offer it some food or water, and, when you have need of the plant, ask it if it is okay to harvest some for your use. Tell it what you wish to use it for, and see how it responds. Only take a small portion of what is available: no more than a third of the overall plant. You must leave enough for the plant to not only survive but thrive. As well, others may be dependent on the plant's gifts, such as insects and animals.

Not everyone can walk outside their door and have easy access to plants. Those living in cities can most certainly work daily with plants, but it may be ones that they grow themselves on windowsills, balconies, and window

---

42 Khait et al., "Sound Perception in Plants."

boxes, as well as a variety of indoor houseplants. Wherever you are, you can always bring plants into your life.

Before working with any plant, ensure that it is safe to handle. Some plants are very toxic and can kill just via handling. There have been deaths and illness and injury in my local area from people mishandling water hemlock and giant hogweed. Some plants look very similar to others, such as water hemlock and alexanders. Confusing the two could be fatal (and has been for two unfortunate souls not far from my home). Try to find a qualified herbalist in your area, if possible, or a local expert in foraging. More and more people are offering classes in these areas, and it's a good idea to see what your community has to offer in this respect. Never, ever ingest a plant that is unknown to you.

Important Note

When using plants medicinally, we are usually taking them internally. We can also do the same in a magical practice. First and foremost, we need to ensure that we are taking the right quantities. Again, consult a qualified herbalist, as they will be able to tell you the correct amounts for what it is that you need. Each person is different, so quantities will vary. As well, certain medications may react very badly to some herbs, causing illness and even death. I cannot say this enough: a qualified herbalist is a necessity.

• • •

There are a couple rules of thumb for working with herbs, which I will share below, but it is your responsibility to find out exactly what works for you in regard to proper guidance and supervision.

Foraging

When foraging your herbs in the wild, it is of utmost importance that you know what you are doing. This means good plant identification as well as good foraging techniques. The best way to really learn how to forage your own wild and hedgerow herbs is to consult a real person, such as a witch, wildcrafter, qualified botanist or herbalist who really knows their stuff. For this kind of skill (working with herbs), there really is no substitution for learning face to face. This is for safety's sake as well as for the protection of the herbs themselves. Bad foraging practices can seriously harm an area's plant life.

Here are ten basic tips for foraging:

- Find someone who knows their stuff and learn from them directly out in the local ecosystem.

- Don't collect any plants from roadsides or near houses, farmer's fields, or industrial areas. These places can be contaminated with all sorts of nasty pollutants, herbicides, and pesticides.

- Forage only where you are allowed to legally. If you are on someone's land, be sure to ask their permission.

- Ensure that what you are foraging is legal. There are many plants that are illegal to take home with you and that are protected by law.

- If there are only a few plants that you desire in a given area, try to find a place where they grow more abundantly. If you can't, try to grow some in your own garden or in containers. Do not forage when there isn't an abundance of the plant.

- Do the least amount of harm. If only taking parts of the plant, ensure that you leave enough growth for the plant to still thrive. If you are going to kill the plant—perhaps by taking it up by the root because that's the part you need in your work—ensure that there are a good amount of other plants of this same kind in the area. A good idea is to collect the seeds beforehand of plants you want to uproot, and scatter them back in the area where you took the plant.

- Avoid harvesting the biggest plants in an area; you will want to ensure that the genetic material from these strong specimens continues. As well, the larger plants tend to have a more varied ecosystem living on, with, or around them.

- Leave the area in good condition. If uprooting a plant, ensure that the soil is replaced. Give some water, if needed, to the other plants around. Scatter seeds of the same plant in the area as mentioned above.

- Use good tools to forage: sharp secateurs, a sharp knife, a hand spade, a trowel, and containers or baskets for collecting.

- Label the plants as you harvest them. If that's not possible, as soon as you get home, include information such as where, when, and how they were collected. This information might come in handy in the future, as well as help you keep track of what you have harvested.

. . .

Let's now take a look at the basics of working with herbs.

Infusions

First of all, I must reinforce that it is highly recommended you talk to a qualified herbalist who can give you the correct herbal allies as well as the correct dosage for a condition. Some people may require more or less in dosages, in larger or smaller concentrations, for example. A qualified herbalist will also be able to determine if any herb has contraindications with existing medicines (Western medicine or any other alternative medicines or therapies), which is a very important thing to consider. **Herbs are powerful allies, and not all herbs work well either together or with pharmaceutical drugs. Some that appear harmless can have very harmful reactions.**

Infusions are the easiest herbal preparations to make. Your basic tea is an infusion. An infusion is simply herbs steeped in water. It's a great way to use dried herbs as water brings them back to life, drawing out their taste, scent, and healing properties. Infusions are used for the aerial parts of plants (the bits that grow above ground). A decoction (described in a following section) is used for roots.

You can make a hot infusion or a cold infusion. A cold infusion usually uses room temperature water, whereas a hot infusion uses boiling water or water than has just boiled and perhaps left a minute or two (depending on the herb). As tea lovers will know, some teas work and taste better when the boiling point has dropped off a bit. When making a hot infusion, it's good to use something that has a lid, like a teapot or a jam jar. This ensures that the steam, which can carry some of the goodness of the herbal properties, including essential oils, is kept within the infusion. It will steam against the lid and then fall back down into the liquid.

As a general rule, an infusion consists of one to two teaspoons dried herb to one cup water. This amount can vary, however, depending upon the condition, the size of the patient, the age of the patient, and a variety of other factors including prescription and over the counter medications. Consult a qualified herbal practitioner!

When making a hot tea, infuse the herbs for 20–30 minutes. You can steep for longer, even overnight, if you require a very strong extract. Refrigerate the infusion afterwards so that it will stay fresh and you can drink it throughout the day as per the recommended dose. For cold infusions, leave a couple of hours to overnight.

Infusions are best made on the day and consumed that same day. Master herbalist Ellen Evert Hopman recommends an adult take ¼ cup four times a day, not with meals, and for children to receive ⅛ cup; breastfeeding infants can ingest through the mother's breastmilk.[43]

Tea balls and reusable tea bags don't really allow the water to reach as much of the herb as possible, so let the herb or herbs float loose in the water in order to ensure that as much contact is made and the properties are fully extracted. Then simply strain with a fine stainless-steel strainer or even a muslin cloth.

43 Hopman, *A Druid's Herbal*, 14.

Decoctions

A decoction is another water-based method of extracting herbal properties from plants, usually roots but sometimes also seeds, berries, and tree bark. As these are tougher than the aerial parts of a plant, they require simmering in a pot on the stove and take more effort than the simpler infusion.

Chop up the material as well as you can, which will release more of its goodness into the water than if you simmered it whole. By increasing the surface area water can reach, you'll get better results. The ratio is similar to an infusion.

Place the herb into the water and bring to a boil, then reduce the heat so that it simmers. Simmering time will vary depending on the herb. Some herbs take less time to extract into the water than others, and working with particularly fibrous parts of a plant will require a good eye and experience. Work with and consult a master herbalist, take some courses, and learn from them directly is always my number one piece of advice to any budding herbalist.

Folk herbalist Corinne Boyer suggests letting a decoction steep after taking it off the heat for an equal amount of time that it simmered. A lot of medicinal strength may be lost if strained too early.[44]

When making infusions or decoctions, use glass, ceramic, or, in the case of simmering a decoction, stainless steel or enamelled pots. Pots that are made of copper, iron, or that contain aluminium or a nonstick coating may contaminate the product with unwanted chemicals and minerals, some of which, as in the case of aluminium, may lead to health problems in the future. Use a stainless-steel sieve to catch out all the bits before ingesting.

Infused Oils

You can make an infused oil by simply stuffing a jar with a fresh herb and pouring oil over it. Good oils to use are extra virgin olive oil or jojoba as they don't go rancid easily like other oils can. Ensure that all plant material is covered with the oil and then leave it in a dark or sunny spot, dependent

---

44 Boyer, *Under the Bramble Arch*, 234.

upon the herb. Some herbs respond to extraction into the oil via sunlight, like St. John's wort. Others need a cool, dark place to sit for a time. It's a good idea to crush or bruise the herbs first to help them release their properties into the oils. Shaking the jar every couple of days also helps the extraction process. The amount of time you require for the extraction depends on the herb, but generally a week or two works. When the oil is ready, simply filter out the vegetable matter and bottle the oil. Some herbal oils are great for applying to the skin or using in the bath. Some are great on salads and add a culinary aspect as well as a magical kick. You can also use an infused oil in the making of your creams. If you want to make a stronger oil, filter out the plant material and pour the semi-finished oil over new plant material, repeating the process until you have the desired outcome.

Salves, Ointments, and Creams

What's the difference between a salve, an ointment, and a cream? Well, a salve is a thick oil and wax preparation that is usually used on a small area, such as lip salve, insect bites and stings, or a localised rash. An ointment is thinner and can be applied to larger areas of the body, such as a vapour rub over the whole chest. Essentially, the oil is emulsified with wax, such as beeswax. The more wax you put in, the thicker it will become. A cream is a mixture of oil and water with an emulsifier such as beeswax or emulsifying wax. At first the art of making creams may seem daunting, but trial and error will get you the results you desire. Remember that what doesn't work can be our greatest teacher!

As a guideline, ointments are generally around 25 grams beeswax to 300 millilitres (10 fluid ounces) of infused oil. Melt the wax in a bain marie (a bowl placed over a pot of boiling water) and add the oil, stirring gently. Add your herbs however you've prepared them (tincture, infusion, decoction, whole, oil, vinegar). Pour into sterilised glass containers and let cool. For a salve, simply add more wax. This is not an exact science, and you will have to go through a process of trial and error to find out exactly which oil and wax combinations work the best for your final product.

A general rule of thumb for creams is 40 millilitres (1.4 fluid ounces) infused oil to eight teaspoons wax. Sometimes a little less wax is needed; again, it depends on the oil that you are using and the type of wax. Some use a combination of both beeswax and emulsifying wax, such as six teaspoons emulsifying wax and two teaspoons beeswax. Beeswax creates a barrier on the skin, so a mix of the two different waxes will allow better penetration. Melt the wax in a bain marie, add the oil, and very slowly pour in 250 millilitres (8.5 fluid ounces) of warm water while briskly whisking away. If you've ever made mayonnaise, you'll know what I'm talking about here! Turn off the heat and remove the pan, keep whisking, and watch as the cream starts to appear. When you've got a cream-like consistency, you can add some essential oils, such as lavender, which act as a preservative. Only two or three drops are needed; first ensure that the essential oil you are using can be used directly on the skin (most aren't suitable, but lavender is; check with an herbalist). Spoon the cream into sterilised jars with well-fitting lids and keep in the refrigerator, where they can last two to three months.

Vinegars

Like oils, properties can be extracted using vinegar. In fact, some plants respond better to the acid in vinegar in the extraction process. They can be used in cooking, in the bath, medicinally, and magically.

Herbal Honeys

You can create honey infusions much the same as the oils and vinegars above. These are particularly helpful in making medicines for coughs and sore throats, as the honey eases the inflamed area of the throat and also has antibiotic and antiseptic properties. You can also make tinctures and then add them to honey to make an herbal honey.

Tinctures

A tincture is an herbal extraction through a high-percentage alcohol rather than oil or vinegar. Alcohol can draw out properties from plant material that other methods may not be able to achieve. Vodka or brandy is generally used, but I prefer to use gin simply for the taste. To create a tincture, a general rule is a half cup dried herbs (double that if using fresh herbs) and two cups of your chosen alcohol, ensuring that the plant matter is totally covered. Store in a cool, dark place for around two weeks, and try to shake daily. Strain out and store in a dark bottle to protect the herbal properties contained in the alcohol. Tinctures only use a couple drops of the preparation at a time, either neat or combined with another liquid or even used in a bath. Dosages will depend on the use, whether ingested or not, the individual in question, medications, and other factors.

Flower Essences

Where the above preparations are used mainly for medicinal purposes, flower essences are used for spiritual means. As mind, body, and soul are connected, working with flower essences can be a powerful and beneficial part of your herbal practice. Making a flower essence could not be any easier. Simply pour clean drinking water into a bowl and take it outside to the plant that you wish to work with. Sit near the plant and commune with it, asking it to lend its properties to your work. Tell it what you wish to do with the energy received. If the plant is willing to share its energy, place the bowl of water under the plant, or if the plant has trailing or drooping stems, you can lean these over the rim of the bowl until the plant is in contact with the water. If you intend to consume this preparation, only use harmless plants that can be internally ingested. If the herb is plentiful in the area and agrees to be cut, you can cut a handful to place into the bowl. Doing this on a sunny day or under a full moon is a great way to boost the powers of the plant.

Leave the plant to send its energies into the water for a couple of hours and then, with thanks, remove the plant from the water without touching the water with your fingers: you can use a twig or even chopsticks or tweezers if necessary. Wood is preferable. Half fill a bottle with brandy, vodka, or gin, and then pour in the flower essence. This will become your mother essence. From the mother essence, you can make smaller 10 millilitres (0.3 fluid ounce) bottles that you can carry with you on your person. Simply fill the small bottle with equal parts water and brandy, vodka, or gin and add three to five drops of your mother essence. Shake it and then it is ready for use. You can use this in creams and lotions, in the bath, or take it internally by placing a few drops under the tongue.

Lustral Baths

Lustral baths are often used prior to a magical working or ritual. They are a great way to get into the proper mindset for magical work and can help ease your mind, body, and soul from the stresses of everyday life, bringing you into a more magical state.

Herbs that are good for use in a lustral bath are mugwort, agrimony, rosemary, lavender, and rose. Make a tea with the herbs, using one teaspoon of herb per cup of water. Combining three herbs uses the magical power of the number three. Or if you have a specific purpose on mind for your ritual or magical working, then you can use the appropriate herb.

AGRIMONY: cleanses the body, mind, and soul

MUGWORT: purifier, psychic inducer

ROSEMARY: purifies and protects

LAVENDER: releases tension, promotes peace

ROSE: calming, loving, self-worth

Pour a few cups of the tea into the bathwater. You can also strew with some of the herbs—just ensure that you've got a good drain cover to stop them from clogging up the drain when you release the water after your bath.

Before getting into the water, you can trace a protective or magical symbol on the water's surface with your dominant hand. It could be a pentagram, the awen (a Druid symbol), a triquetra or triskele, or a heart for love. Think on what you are trying to achieve with your work and put that energy into every aspect of it, including your lustral bath.

If you don't have access to a bathtub, you can still make the tea and place it in a nice bowl. Once it has cooled to room temperature, take a shower.

At the end of your shower, pour the contents of the bowl over your head and let it slide down your body. You can trace a symbol for your work onto the water in the bowl beforehand, for added power and energy. Feel it infusing your body as you pour it over yourself and allow it to run down your skin. A light rinse afterwards, and you're good to go.

Washing away the day's work or any stress or tension in mind, body, and spirit can help you immensely in your magical or spiritual work. It allows you to reset and come back to the work in a new frame of mind: a more magical mind.

• • •

Now let's look at some more herbs for the hedge witch. The herbs listed below are local to my area and may not be available in your part of the world. You can always try to find local herbs that have similar properties and magical correspondences. One of the hedge witch's mottos is use what you've got!

Agrimony (Agrimonia Eupatoria)

With its small yellow star-shaped flowers, agrimony is native to the British Isles and was brought over to North America. It is a perennial, enjoying meadows, pastureland, and other grassy areas. It is a member of the Rosaceae family.

Use the flowers and leaves, discarding the stems. Medicinally it is a very good healer of wounds, first by stopping the bleeding and cleansing the wound, then by aiding the healing afterwards. It also is a good pain reliever. As an astringent, it tightens and tones the tissues of the body. The tea is also a good eyewash for conditions such as conjunctivitis. Its astringent properties help reduce inflammation, which works well in poultices for sprains and strains. It also helps with stomach complaints such as diarrhoea and IBS. It can also treat jaundice and other liver conditions. It treats chronic cystitis and irritable bladder syndrome and helps to prevent urinary leakage at any age. Its astringent properties are also good for those who do a lot of public speaking or singing, as it clears the throat of excess phlegm.

It's also good for clearing up bouts of constipation and diarrhoea, releasing undo tension, and helping things flow better.

Historically, it was said to be used to treat snakebite; this is not recommended. However, it can be used for insect bites and stings. Perhaps the snake was a reference to the Druids, who also used "adder stones" and had other serpentine associations. The Gaelic name for agrimony is *mur-druidheann*, meaning "sorrow of the Druids."[45] This is thought to relate to agrimony's use in dispelling lethargy and depression. The Anglo-Saxons used it to heal wounds, using the name *garclive* or *gár-clife*.[46]

As an astringent, agrimony helps reset the nervous system, relaxing tension in the body and alleviating stress in both the mind and the body. The tincture is especially good for this. You can also put the tincture directly on a burn and take a few drops internally to help ease the pain.

Magically, agrimony is used for psychic cleansing and protection. It works as a counter-magic herb and can help shield against any sort of magical attack. Charge it with protective energy and wear it in a small bag as a talisman. Burn it as an incense or use it to cleanse your altar or sacred work or living space. Making a tea to drink beforehand, and then another cup for the bath water itself, can help cleanse and purify the body and the soul. Pain, either physical or mental, can be related to constriction, and agrimony helps to ease that, allowing tension to dissolve.

Beech (Fagus Sylvatica)

Beech is a tree that, for some reason, often gets overlooked in many modern and magical herbals. It is not part of the Druid tree ogham (a magical tree alphabet), and it rarely shows up in other Pagan herbals. As an indigenous British tree, I feel that we need to include the beech once again in our herbal grimoires and honour this most beautiful and magnificent being.

---

45 "Thirteen Uses of Plants in Druidry," OBOD, https://druidry.org/druid-way/teaching-and-practice/druid-plant-lore (accessed February 19, 2024).

46 Middle English Compendium, University of Michigan library, https://quod.lib.umich.edu/m/middle-english-dictionary/dictionary/MED18188 (accessed February 19, 2024).

According to the seminal 1931 herbal by Mrs. M. Grieve simply known as *A Modern Herbal*, the word *beech* is thought to derive from the Germanic language and refers to the word "book."[47] It's thought that early books were made from beech. Maybe this is why the Druids didn't include it in their tree ogham? As members of an oral tradition, this might be one use that they're not terribly comfortable with!

It's one of our largest and most gorgeous trees. It spreads its canopy and isn't afraid to shine. In the autumn especially we see its enchanting beauty as the chlorophyll retreats and the golden leaves begin to glow in the late slanting sunlight. They then turn a beautiful rust colour if they're not blown away by the autumn winds. The pale grey, smooth trunks stand in silent glory, with little to no undergrowth beneath them to mar their stately splendour. They are truly magical beings, and these majestic and proud trees always make me think of the Fair Folk of the elven wood of Lothlorien in Tolkien's work *The Lord of the Rings*.

Beechwood was often used in the making of chairs, wooden panels for furniture, carpenter's planes, and charcoal for gunpowder. But it's not just the wood that is useful: the nuts (mast) were very valuable for owners of livestock who grazed their animals in the woods and under these trees on the village common. Like acorns, beech nuts are very nutritious for pigs, and the wild deer, squirrels, and badgers are also very fond of them. The whole nuts are not good for human consumption, but the oil extracted from them is used in cooking in Europe. You can also use the oil as a furniture polish.

The tar has been used medicinally as an antiseptic and also for treating chronic bronchitis. You can also make a liqueur from the young leaves (pick them before midsummer). An easy recipe is to simply fill a jar with beech leaves, top up with your favourite spirit (for me, that's gin), and leave for ten days. Then add a pound of sugar per pint of spirit, dissolving the sugar over a low heat but being careful not to boil off the alcohol. Bottle, let it sit for three months to a year, strain, and enjoy!

47 Grieve, *A Modern Herbal*, 92.

For magical purposes, beech can be used in spells to enhance one's appearance or in spells that call for strength, grace, or adaptability. You can use beech to consecrate a grimoire of any kind, such as your own herbal grimoire, or even better, use slats of beechwood as the covers! I also think that beech is a great tree to connect to the Fair Folk, though this is from personal experience and not something that is written down in any lore.

Borage (Borago Officinalis)

Borage is a great herbal ally for women's health. I understood this as I started getting hot flushes from menopause. My garden usually provides me medically with a proliferation of a certain herb when I feel any disease. During a series of hot flushes that lasted for weeks (around four per hour), I went out into the garden and paid attention to what my garden was telling me. In the midst of a fairly barren garden in March, borage was blooming in several places. The early bees loved it as much as I did, but for different reasons.

It was only after I started drinking borage tea from my garden that I discovered it helped to produce oestrogen/progesterone during the menopausal years. Borage contains gamma-linoleic acid, or omega-6 fatty acid, even more so than evening primrose oil. It also helps support the adrenal glands, acting as a nervine tonic. As such, it helps with stressful situations during emotional times in one's life. However, one shouldn't take borage over a very long period as it can affect the liver as well as thin the blood. Borage also contains pyrrolizine, which is carcinogenic and mutagenic, so the advice is to use it only sparingly.[48] Borage seed oil usually eliminates the harmful chemical in the processing stage, but double check the label to ensure that it is certified free of toxic unsaturated pyrrolizidine alkaloids.

Borage is known as the "herb of gladness" from the Gaelic word *borrach*, meaning person of courage or bravery.[49] It is said that Celtic warriors used it before battle to strengthen themselves. There is an old adage that comes along with this herb: "borage for courage." Borage flowers are

48 Kúnkele et al., *Herbs for Healthy Living*, 77.
49 McGarry, *Brighid's Healing*, 181.

a wonderful addition to spring and summer salads, and the leaves can be cooked like spinach. Borage has a slight cucumber taste to it. The leaves and stems can get very bristly hairs growing on them, so cooking is best to soften and remove these before ingestion. You can also juice the leaves and stalks. You can use borage as a tea with the leaves and flowers or in a salad, as previously mentioned. You can also make borage wine (for a great recipe, see Anna Franklin's *The Hearth Witch's Compendium*).[50]

Borage grows best in poor soil. We never planted any of our borage; it just came into the garden on its own. Well-drained soil is best, in a very sunny aspect. It is originally a Mediterranean herb.

Magically speaking, you can use the herb in spells to strengthen your courage or see you through a difficult time. Strewing some leaves and flowers around the base of a candle, charging the candle with your intent, and then burning it throughout the difficult time can help ease the pain and suffering or provide you with what you need to cope and get through. Borage is also good for spells to begin a new project. It is an herb associated with the festival of Lughnasadh and is ideal to serve up as part of the ritual feast. You can also use borage for meditations and to promote psychic awareness through burning as an incense.

Burdock (Arctium Lappa)

If you grew up in an area where there was burdock, you've probably thrown or had the burrs attach to your clothing. It's said that these burrs were the inspiration for Velcro! The hooks get stuck on the loops of clothing or in the fur of animals, which is a great way for the plant to spread its seed across a wider area.

As a biennial, it takes two years to complete a full cycle of growth to seed. It has a long, deep taproot that is difficult to access, as it can grow up to a metre down into the ground! You can use the leaves, the root, and the seeds. The flowers that resemble thistles are what turn into the ubiquitous burrs in the autumn months. In folklore these burrs are known as beggar's buttons.

50 Franklin, *The Hearth Witch's Compendium*, 84.

The word "burr" comes from the Latin *burre*, meaning a shank of wool, in which burrs were commonly found on sheep. You can find burdock on roadsides, wastelands, field edges, hedgerows, and forest edges. The root is often used in Asian cooking and is high in vitamin C.

Here in the UK, you can still buy traditional dandelion and burdock soda. I would not advise buying the versions offered by large companies and supermarkets and instead look out for the real versions that actually contain the plants described and not synthetic ingredients mixed with a lot of sugar. These are usually available in glass bottles from small companies and have an old-fashioned look to them. Better yet, make your own! It is delicious served chilled on a hot summer's day.

Burdock has a long history of use in Europe. Its use as an immune booster is well known, but did you know that it has been used to treat cancer in the early twelfth century, leprosy and syphilis in the Middle Ages, and HIV in modern times? It's also a great blood purifier. When combined with dandelion's diuretic properties, you can really give your system a good internal cleansing.

Burdock leaves are great for skin complaints too, such as acne, bruises, and boils. A poultice applied to the skin will calm it down and bring relief. Steam the leaf until soft and then apply it hot to the area. Keep a hot water bottle over it to hold in the warmth for around twenty minutes to half an hour. You can also use the same for arthritis and rheumatism. Combine the root with dandelion in a decoction and you can treat eczema and psoriasis as well.

Magically you can use burdock's spiky burrs to ward off negative energies and protect the home. You can also put it in an amulet bag combined with other items for similar reasons. Use it in spells to increase beauty and attractiveness. It's also good in healing spells of all kinds. Use it in spells for cleansing and purification too, for what it does medicinally, it will also do magically.

Chickweed (Stellaria Media)

Chickweed gets its stellar name from the star-shaped flowers that adorn this very unassuming but very beneficent plant. You will find chickweed growing in hedgerows, your garden, and almost anywhere. It begins to grow around March or April, depending on how cold the winter has been, and runs through until the first sharp frosts.

As its name suggests, chickens love it, but we humans can enjoy it too! Chickweed is a great source of vitamins A and C, and therefore it is very helpful especially in spring when we are a little vitamin deficient after a long winter. It also contains lots of minerals such as iron, calcium, magnesium, and even copper. It's a wonderful spring tonic that is easily harvested. You can adorn salads with it, put it in smoothies, or even make a pesto with it. You can also make teas with it or use it in soups.

Chickweed has long been known for its anti-inflammatory properties. It's very good on rashes and skin irritations such as sunburn or insect bites. You can use it on bruises, sprains, and other injuries. In emergencies, just pull up a handful, chew it up, and then place the makeshift poultice on the area. It's also great for other skin conditions such as eczema and shingles. Combine chickweed with chamomile or plantain for a great skin-soothing ointment.

Chickweed is also a mild diuretic, so it is sometimes used in weight-loss products. A better use for this diuretic action would be to relieve kidney stones.

The high saponin level of chickweed means that it is a great boost for the internal organs, allowing them to function at their highest levels.[51] You can also use it for coughs and colds, sore throats, and other respiratory ailments. For thousands of years, it has been used for eye inflammations.

Magically speaking, chickweed can be used in healing spells of all kinds. It's also a great spell component when you need to cool something down. You can use it in love and fertility magic (it grows and spreads rapidly in the wild). According to British witch and author Anna Franklin, it is associated with the goddess Brigantia.

The plant's white and green colours tie in nicely with the festival of Imbolc, so should you be lucky enough to live in a climate where chickweed is around at this time, it can make a wonderful addition to any ritual.

---

51 Bruton-Seal et al., *Hedgerow Medicine*, 28.

You can also make a flower essence with it for magical work. The floppiness of the plant means that you can just tuck a bowl underneath and drape some flowering stems into the water, letting the essence fill it with all its energetic beauty without harming the plant.

Cleavers (Galium Aparine)

A great springtime herb, cleavers is an often overlooked plant that has really important properties. In the past it was greatly praised as a spring tonic, but sadly today the wisdom is being lost. The famed Welsh Physicians of Myddfai in the thirteenth century praised cleavers for its powers to make one strong and healthy. A small patch of cleavers, like nettles in your garden, can be a great ally in your physical and spiritual health. Found along roadsides, bridleways, streams and riverbanks, footpaths, in hedgerows and in gardens, cleavers is a hardy plant that begins to grow in the late winter months.

Cleavers boosts the lymphatic system, which essentially cleanses the body and blood. It's also known to shrink tumours. Cleavers supports the urinary tract and is good for treating cystitis, kidney inflammation and stones, irritable bladder, and urethritis.

Cleavers is otherwise known as sticky willy or goosegrass, and many a person has been foraging in a hedgerow only to come home and find a strand of cleavers stuck to part of their clothing. Gather the plant until it starts to flower: after flowering it becomes a bit tough, the spines becoming harder and unsuitable for taking internally. When it first appears, you can eat it straight in a salad as a lovely spring green by chopping it finely and sprinkling over other greens. You can also put it in a salad dressing. Gather the plant and pop into a blender with some water, blitz it up, and strain out the juice for a lovely healthy green drink. You can make a syrup by combining cleavers juice with equal parts honey and vegetable glycerine, which will keep for months, enabling you to drink it throughout the year. Take a teaspoon or two several times a day for a healthy boost, to get rid of fluid retention, for urinary problems, and also for breast cysts. In late summer and autumn, the seeds can be gathered up to be used as a coffee substitute, and the root can be used as a plant dye with a lovely shade of red, for cleavers is of the Madder family.

You can also use cleavers to soothe skin complaints such as rashes, burns, or blisters. A poultice of the crushed plant can be applied directly to the skin. Again, use the young plant for this. An ointment helps to relieve dry skin, and a salve is great for chapped lips and burns.

Use cleavers for spells that involve rebirth and renewal, especially in the spring. You can also use it for purification by burning it on an incense block and using it to fumigate. The sticky spines of the plant are great in spells of attraction, so if you'd like to draw something to you that will stick, this is the plant to use! It can also help aid your willpower by helping you stick to your goals.

Meadowsweet (Filipendula Ulmaria)

Meadowsweet was an important herb to the Celts and the Germanic peoples. It was used medicinally as well as for culinary purposes, and it was also featured in Bronze Age burials across Britain, as can be seen from pollen samples collected from archaeological sites such as the Orkneys in Scotland down to Carmarthenshire in Wales.

Meadowsweet is probably best known for its properties as a painkiller. It contains acetylsalicylic acid, much like willow bark from which the modern-day aspirin is derived. It also reduces fever and treats diarrhoea and stomach acid problems, unlike aspirin, which can aggravate stomach conditions and affect the lining if taken too often. Herbs taken in their whole form are often much better for the human body to consume, as holistically the chemical compounds work together to bring healing. When a single compound such as the salicin is extracted and turned into aspirin, the benefits or balancing properties of the plant's other elements (such as flavonoids) cannot work with it to create balance. Therefore, we see the side effects that aspirin has on the body as opposed to meadowsweet in its whole form.

A lesser-known healing property of meadowsweet is for cystitis and urethritis. It can also be used to break down kidney stones and gravel and treat gout. It is a strong toxin eliminator and dispels uric acid from the body.

The name *meadowsweet* most likely comes from the fact that it was used in making mead as opposed to growing in meadows. It has also been used to flavour beer and wine as well as the production of syrups. It was also used to cure depression and can be used as an eyewash. It treats rheumatic complaints and achiness from the flu.

The Druids are said to have used meadowsweet to cure malaria as well as in a febrifuge, which promotes sweating to reduce a fever. Its Gaelic name is *belt of Cuchulainn*, as it was given to the hero in one of the legends to cure a fever. It was also one of the plants used to create the lovely flower maiden Blodeuwedd in Welsh lore. Meadowsweet was also used as a strewing herb, meaning that it was strewn across an earthen floor to scent a room and make it more pleasant. It has an almond/marzipan smell that is lovely. It is said that meadowsweet was one of the three most important herbs of the Druids alongside vervain and watermint. Meadowsweet might be an herb of the goddess Brighid, for one of its folk names is bridewort (*Bride* being another name for Brighid).

You can simmer the flowering heads in wine or make a tea with two tablespoons in one cup liquid. Drink slowly throughout the day, a quarter at a time. For a stronger effect, and to use for fevers, the root is better in the same quantity. Magically, use meadowsweet in funerary rites or other rites of passage, such as in a bridal bouquet. You can also use it to switch from one situation into another to break a cycle.

Mistletoe (Viscum Album)

The Druids are famed for cutting the mistletoe on the sixth day of the new moon, as recorded by Pliny. This ritual was depicted in various nineteenth-century paintings such as *The Druidess* by Armand Laroche and *Druids Cutting the Mistletoe* by Henri-Paul Motte. The ritual described by Pliny states that a golden knife or sickle was used to cut mistletoe from the tree, and it was not allowed to touch the ground but rather was caught in a white cloth before it hit the ground. This is because mistletoe is a parasitic plant that lives high above the ground in the branches of its host. It is thus connected to air and light and is often used in midwinter celebrations not only because it is highly visible at this time of year, but because it represents the return of the light, fertility, and holiness.

In his work *Natural History*, Pliny states:

> The Druids, for so call they their Magi, have nothing more sacred than the mistletoe, and the tree on which it grows, provided it be the oak. They select a particular grove of oaks and perform no sacred rites without oak leaves, so that from this custom they may seem to have been called Druids (Oakites), according to the Greek interpretation of that word. They reckon whatever grows on these trees is sent down from Heaven and a proof that the tree itself is chosen by Deity. But the mistletoe is very rarely found and when found is sought after with the greatest religious ardour, and principally in the sixth moon, which is the beginning of their months and years, and when the tree is thirty years old it is then not half grown only but has attained its full vigour. They call it All Heal (Ull-ice) by a word in their own language and having proper sacrifices and feasts under the trees with great solemnity bring up two white bulls, whose horns are first bound. The priest, clothed in a white surplice, ascends the tree and cuts it off with a golden knife, and it is received in a white sheet. Then they sacrifice the victims (bulls) and pray that God would render his own gifts prosperous to those on whom he has bestowed it. They reckon the mistletoe administered as a potion can impart fecundity to any barren animal and that it is a remedy against all kinds of poison.[52]

The white berries of the mistletoe contain a sticky juice that closely resembles semen, which connects it to fertility. The berries are poisonous, so please do not come into physical contact with them. The knife or sickle that the Druids are purported to have used is probably a highly polished bronze blade or perhaps even brass, as gold is not strong enough to carry a sharp edge for cutting.

Apple is mistletoe's favoured tree to grow on, although it grows on many different trees like birch. The Druid ritual speaks of it growing in oak trees; however, this is very rare, so if you see mistletoe on an oak, consider yourself doubly lucky! Where I live, we often see mistletoe growing around

---

52   Pliny, *Historia Naturalis*.

areas of healing, such as in the trees around Ipswich hospital or the huge ball of mistletoe high in a birch tree right next to the pharmacy across from my dentist's office! Another interesting thing to note is that mistletoe can have flowers and fruit all on the same plant: it seems to defy the natural progression that other plants follow in the cycle of the seasons. It will often appear as a big ball in the branches of a tree, growing every which way and not necessarily toward the light.

Some mistletoe turns a golden colour in the winter; hence, it is sometimes called the golden bough. The leaves and twigs are used medicinally, although they should only be used by a qualified practitioner as dosage is extremely important. This is a very, very potent plant and can cause severe illness and even death if used incorrectly. As well, the host plant that it grows on affects its own qualities and uses. The American mistletoe (*Phoradendron flavenscens*) closely resembles the European mistletoe.

Magically, mistletoe can be used in spells of healing (for its name "All Heal") and for luck, divination, and fertility. It is also often used in Yuletide rites and rituals alongside holly, ivy, and other evergreens. Remember, if you are going to decorate your home with real mistletoe, wear gloves and keep it out of reach of pets and children.

Self-Heal (Prunella Vulgaris)

Self-heal is abundant in grassy meadows, woods, and even lawns. It is found almost everywhere on the planet and is a great herbal ally to have. The flowers and leaves are used in herbal preparations. Some cultures say to gather the flowers when in full bloom, others when they are first starting to wilt and brown.

The antiviral properties of self-heal have made it a great healer historically for ulcers of all kinds, from mouth ulcers to those found in more private regions of the body due to a sexually transmitted disease. Today it is used for treating colds and flu. Self-heal helps the body to self-regulate and therefore is great for thyroid conditions as well as for the symptoms of menopause.

It is anti-inflammatory as well as a great immune booster. Apply it as a salve or ointment in order to speed up the wound healing process. It can also help ease the aches and pains of arthritis and similar conditions in the same manner.

Teas, oils, creams: this herb is very versatile when used medicinally. It also makes a wonderful flower essence.

Magically, this plant is extremely useful in healing rituals and spells of all kinds. You can work with the flower essence or take in a lustral bath. Burn some as an incense or create a misting spray with the essence to spray around a sick person's room and promote healing in any capacity. Listen to what the plant has to tell you; it will share the best way forward for its use. Use it for emotional healing as well as to help heal mental trauma. When used in meditation and prayer, it opens up the heart to receive the healing messages from the divine.

I am always surprised that self-heal features so little in Pagan herbals and grimoires. This little herb is such a great ally to have, so abundantly available worldwide—often right under our noses—and yet used so very little. Perhaps this is a reflection of our times, where we often don't see the true beauty and benefits that are right there in front of us.

Plants in the Home

The hedge witch doesn't only work with the wild things growing in her local landscape, but also takes care to bring the green and growing things into her home. There are many houseplants that even the blackest of thumbs could take care of; here I will list some of my favourites that are hardy and hardworking in the home for both magical and mundane reasons.

For me, a home is not a home without plants. As I have asthma, I have many plants that help clean the air as well as plants that have been "inherited" from people at my husband's work who moved offices and didn't take their plants with them. These are all now a part of the family.

First off, we have peace lilies, which are super easy to take care of. They exude peace into the home. They start to droop when they need water, and then when watered they perk right back up. They're very easy to take care of because they tell you what they need, although you should try to keep them watered and not let them dry out and droop as doing this too much stresses the plant and weakens it. Always put peace lilies in places where cats will not get any pollen from the flowers on them as it is poisonous to them and other pets.

Ivy is another great household plant. I took an ivy cutting from my garden, where it was growing across the stairs and would eventually create a trip hazard. I brought a cutting indoors in the hopes of rooting it and then planting it (which it did nicely). To root an ivy cutting, just place it in a glass of water where the water covers the stem from beneath the bottom-most leaf. Place it in a sunny windowsill for a few weeks or a couple of months, and watch as small roots begin to grow from the stem in the water. Keep the water clean and topped up. When you have a good root system going, you can then transfer it to a pot of soil. Keep it moist but not over-watered for the first month. Ivy is a great ally for good health.

Mother-in-law's tongue, also known as snake plant, is an amazing plant. We now have five that have all came from one single, small plant. It needs separating when it starts to outgrow its pot, and soon it will be in every room in the house! This is a very hardy plant that can stand overwatering and underwatering, though you really should try to avoid these situations in the first place. This is a good protection plant to keep away negative influences (and perhaps mothers-in-law).

Ah, ficus; a plant that needs minimal fuss. Just please don't overwater them. All of the ficuses in our house started life as desk plants when I used to work as a legal secretary about eighteen years ago. I kept repotting them into bigger and bigger pots, and now they are small trees, great for my ritual/mediation room where I perform most of my hedge riding. They are a great makeshift hedgerow in your house: my ritual room is surrounded by three 5-foot ficuses that act in such a capacity. Ficuses are great to help promote strength, endurance, and adaptability.

Spider plants are premium air-cleaning plants that again require minimal fuss. I think I have ten in my home, again all coming from one single plant. They flower and then form little perfect baby spider plants that you simply snip off from the stem and then repot! The spider plant is a great plant for purification and proliferation.

Creeping Jenny is another prolific plant that is super easy to propagate. Just cut off a tip with a few leaves on it, stick the stem into some watered compost, and you will soon have another plant! I pot up five little clippings into a pot to help it spread more quickly into a decent-sized plant. These are great for their lush greenery. For some hedge magic, pot up up some cuttings, whisper a charm over them, and allow your intent (such as for abundance and fertility) to come into your life.

Aloe is another great propagator; we have several that have all come from one initial plant. You will find babies growing up right next to the mother in the pot, which you can then repot on its own with no fuss. They like to stay near the mother plant for a while after repotting, I've found, before you can move them to a different room. They need to grow up before moving out and away from mom. Aloe is a great healer, both physically and spiritually.

Cacti are plants of resilience and strength. They are great for bringing solar energy into your home. Mine live in the conservatory, as they're the only things that can endure the heat, sun, and cold winter weather in that room with no central heating. They bloom several times a year and are a joy in the dead of winter, reminding me of the sunnier times to come. Cacti of all kinds are great plants for protection and hardiness.

Devils' ivy (pothos) is sometimes called the money plant. Have it in your home not only because it looks amazing, but also to bring in wealth and abundance. Again, it is a great plant to clean the air in the home.

Don't forget that you can also use dried flowers! Take some from the garden and dry them (I use my airing cupboard for this) to bring their energy and beauty into your home. These little posies are great for promoting peace and love and also just because they are beautiful to have around the home. I also have ears of dried corn (maize) for abundance, as well as dried chili peppers and satsumas for their fiery energy and protection. We also have a Suffolk-made corn dolly in the shape of a horseshoe for good luck.

Bringing plants into your home not only helps boost your magic, but also helps improve your quality of life overall. Take good care of them, and they will take good care of you.

• • •

This is just the beginning of working with plant allies. There are so many good books out there on herbcraft, and do try to see if there are any local classes being offered in your area by a qualified practitioner. Scour the internet to see if there is anyone local to you that offers workshops or even courses to help you qualify. Check the bibliography section of this book and also the suggested reading list below for good herbal books that I use over and over again in my own practice.

SUGGESTED READING

Brighid's Healing: Ireland's Celtic Medicine Traditions by Gina
  McGarry (Green Magic Publishing, 2005)
  A brilliant book with an Irish focus and one of my favourites.
  McGarry's herbal knowledge skills shine throughout the text. She
  also founded a herbal healing academy called Brighid's Academy of
  Healing Arts.[53]

The Green Witch: Your Complete Guide to the Natural Magic of
  Herbs, Flowers, Essential Oils, and More by Arin Murphy-Hiscock
  (Adams Media, 2017)
  A Canadian author whose works are prolific, this volume is
  definitely one to be added to a witch's library. Well-written in an
  easygoing manner, this is also a hardback, which lengthens the
  book's lifespan.

The Hearth Witch's Compendium: Magical and Natural Living for
  Every Day by Anna Franklin (Llewellyn, 2018)
  A wonderful compendium of herbal knowledge, with great recipes.

---

53 Brighids's Academy of Healing Arts, https://brighidsacademy.wordpress.com
    (accessed February 21, 2024).

Hedgerow Medicine: Harvest and Make Your Own Herbal Remedies by Julie Bruton-Seal and Matthew Seal (Merlin Unwin Books, 2008)
An invaluable work that was my first introduction to working with herbs.

Magical Herbalism: The Secret Craft of the Wise by Scott Cunningham (Llewellyn, 2017)
A classic text on the magical uses of herbs.

Wild Witchcraft: A Guide to Natural, Herbal and Earth Magic by Marian Green (Thorsons, 2002)
An older work from one of the seminal Witchcraft authors in the UK, this is filled with wonderful information on how to integrate herb magic into your craft.

The bluebells carpet the floor of the hazel wood. The trees are slowly waking up in the late spring sunshine, but now is the time for the magical little blue flowers to shine. These faery bells exist in a liminal time when it is neither spring nor summer but a combination of both. They dwell in the dappled light of a deciduous forest without leaves, with only the bare branches providing some shade. They smell like the colours blue and purple.

I take a small bowl out of my bag and sit in a patch of vibrant blue, careful not to crush any of the precious blossoms. I can feel the flowers singing to me, enchanting me to come nearer. I pour some water from my bottle into the bowl and place it under the flowers next to me, letting their drooping heads heavy with faery bells lie in the water. I sit and meditate, communing with the flowers and the forest around me. Time passes; bees and flies buzz past me, squirrels scamper up and down the trees. The sun shines softly, and the gentle breeze seems to be awakening everything around me, including my own soul.

When the flowers tell me that they are done, I pull the flower heads out of the water and gently put them back in place. With the rest of the water left in the bottle, I give an offering and say a quiet prayer of gratitude. I tell the flowers what I will be doing with this wonderful gift, and I can feel another energy boost coming from the entirety of the area as a small wave of bluebell energy goes into my work. My eyes fill up with unshed tears at the joy and generousness of the earth, and I let them fall to the earth in benediction.

Chapter 11

Divination and Creating Your Own Practice

Fortune favours the prepared mind.

. . . . . .

Louis Pasteur

Divination can be an essential part of the hedge witch's practice. But just what exactly is divination? Is it just fortunetelling, knowing auspicious times such as when the planets are aligning, or is it something deeper?

Let's first take a moment to look more closely at the word *divination*. The first thing that we see but may not really take in is the word *divine*. We've been so accustomed in our society to see divination as a certain thing that we've forgotten the actual roots of the word and the practice. Divination is to consult and work with the divine. For those who choose not to work with the gods, you can see this as consulting and working with the energy of the universe instead.

So, first and foremost, we are going to bring the divine back into divination in this chapter. If this word bothers you, substitute it as indicated above. It's a really important factor when working this into your witchery. It brings substance to your various methods of divination as well as a return to source.

Dictionary time! Let's see what it has to say regarding the word "divine":

- connected with a god or like a god
- extremely pleasant or enjoyable
- to guess something
- to search for water or minerals underground by holding horizontally in your hands a Y-shaped rod or stick, the end of which suddenly points down slightly when water or minerals are below it

So, the first description relates to the divine. Wonderful! The second makes me smile because connection to the divine can bring about these feelings as well. The third description leaves me a bit cold, really. It's that old academic habit of brushing off magic as "mumbo jumbo"—as if we're just guessing, not working with the gods or the energy of the universe. And the fourth description is interesting as it mentions one of many different divination practices and could be connected to the first. We will look at that more closely later in this chapter.

The Divine in Divination

Bringing the divine into your divination practice can notch it up a whole new level. You may cast the runes, but if you have a connection to Odin or Freya, for instance, and say a prayer to them and feel them flowing through your reading, then you may find that the reading becomes easier to perform, easier to interpret, and that it feels more true and relevant. It can be an act of holy reverence and connection to a deity who is known for a particular divinatory skill, such as Odin and the runes or Freya and the oracular practice of seidr. Connecting to the divine charges a reading, the search for an answer, or just communing with the divine in general, and it adds extra power and energy in order for the person to work in alignment with what the gods are trying to tell us.

To deal with this energy correctly, it helps to prepare the mind first and foremost. If you are going to talk to and consult the gods, it's best to do some housekeeping first. A regular meditation practice helps the mind settle and lets you get out of your own way. I am a huge proponent of the benefits of meditation. Meditation that focuses on the breath for twenty to thirty minutes each and every day can prepare the mind to better receive information more fully from both this world and from other spiritual realms. It's so simple to do, yet it requires us to show up for the practice, daily if possible. Sitting down, finding a comfortable position, and just focusing on the breath is all that it takes. The mind will wander, and when it does, you just bring it back to the breath—again and again and again. It's that persistence, that return to centre, that is the gift of this practice. Far too many people berate themselves for their wandering minds during meditation, but each time it gives us an opportunity to return. That we learn each time we come back to the breath is the lesson itself and the reward. Let that learning go deep into your psyche and your soul. It's not a failure. It's a success that you've returned to yourself each time.

Try to start with a daily mediation practice for a month, and see how you feel. Start with ten or fifteen minutes a day if twenty or thirty minutes feels like too much at once. At the end of each meditation practice, spend five or ten minutes opening yourself up to the deity that you wish to work with, that you feel you want in your life. If you don't work with deity, open yourself up to the energy of the universe and feel it humming both within and without, all around you. You are a part of that energy, with your own vibration and connection. You may notice that doing this after a meditation session brings that energy, whether of a deity or the energy of the universe in general, closer to you. This stays with you throughout the next day or a few days. Send energy back, send love, and you will feel it coming back to you immediately in your session in a big wave of reciprocity because we are all connected, every single thing in this universe. It's such a wonderful experience.

Having the correct frame of mind is essential before embarking upon any form of divination, whether it's using copper rods in the wilderness, a pendulum in your home, or the tarot cards at a psychic fair. A calm open mind is essential. If you are trying to read messages with a flustered, scared, or angry mind, you may very well misinterpret the messages that are trying to reach you. Again, a daily meditative practice will help you in this regard as well as in many other aspects of your emotional, physical, and spiritual well-being.

With the mind settled through a daily mediation practice and nourished through a connection to the divine, it's time to have a conversation with them. In any oracular process, you are having a conversation with the divine. You might have questions or simply wish to see if the path that is currently being taken is correct. You may wish to work for other people, to help them on their life's journey. In any event, you are asking questions, so it's much more beneficial to have an established relationship with a deity or the universe before you go about bothering them with questions. How would you feel if a stranger came up to you and started to ask personal questions? Think of it in this way, and you will see the importance of relationship before asking the divine or the universe to offer up the answers.

Offerings can help deepen the bonds of relationship. Give an offering before or after a reading, whether you are working with tarot, runes, oracle cards, whatever. Send your love and energy back to where you got the information from. Relationship is about reciprocity.

Which Witch Are You?

Before we look at different methods of divination, it is useful to take a look at the skills that you currently have so you can better choose a method that works for you. When we are divining, we are tapping into the energy of the divine (or universal energy) by allowing our psychic minds to open and receive messages that can be interpreted through the reading. Each one of us has psychic ability in varying degrees, which is an ability to read, interpret, and understand information on more than just one level. The good news is that this is a skill that can be worked on in order to gain more proficiency. Let's look at different psychic skills to determine where your strengths may lie.

Perhaps the most well-known psychic skill is that of the clairvoyant. This literally means "clear seeing." The witch gazing into her crystal ball is the stereotypical image of this skill in practice, but there are many other methods through which a clairvoyant can receive messages. Precognisant dreams can fall into the category of the clairvoyant, for example. Have you ever had a dream and then a part or all of it came true? Most everyone has. However, if this happens on a fairly regular basis, then the images in the dreams are speaking to your clear sight. I often dream of things happening in the natural world, such as earthquakes, which then appear on the morning news the next day. I remember one morning after I had dreamt of a stone circle that had been vandalised; when I looked at the papers, they had a story of a stone circle in Scotland that had been desecrated with graffiti during the night. These types of dreams are regular occurrences in my life, and I keep a solid record of them in the form of a dream journal. This helps me better understand my particular skill and improve it. Different phases of the moon, for example, can be tapped into for precognitive dreams, if you show an aptitude at certain moon phases. You will only know if you keep track of your dreams. Having a dream journal and pen next to the bed allows you to record the details of the dream straightaway (which may be forgotten as the day progresses) as well as the time of day/ night and the phase of the moon.

The clairvoyant is naturally talented in visualisation. If this comes easily to you, then you might like to delve deeper in clairvoyancy. If you tend to make eye contact with people in order to better understand them, their feelings, and motivations, you may be clairvoyant. If you enjoy bright colours or well-decorated areas, anywhere that has a nice visual aesthetic, you may be clairvoyant. Is it easier to do something after someone physically shows you? Then you are indeed a visual person, and clairvoyancy might be the method for you.

Clairvoyants are attracted to different scrying methods, as they can literally see shapes, outlines, and sometimes even full-colour moving pictures in objects such as in a dark bowl of water, a dark mirror (a mirror with a black surface), crystals, fire, etc. They are also attracted to very visual forms of divination, such as the tarot and oracle cards.

Clairaudiency is "clear hearing." If you are clairaudient, you might hear other people's thoughts, much like telepathy. Someone might say a word that triggers a knowing deep inside you. Clairaudiency is linked to intuition, as in "listening to your inner voice." You might also hear the voice of a divinity in your work, aiding you and guiding you toward what you need to know. Do you know what someone is going to say before they say it? Does a voice sometimes come to you in need? Does being in a large, crowded, loud environment cause you distress? Does a name pop into your head when the phone rings and you intuitively know who it is? If you are a musician, do you play by ear rather than read music? You may be clauraudient.

Clairaudients may be drawn to any method of divination, hearing the answers rather than paying too much attention to visuals. Sounds in nature can be especially good divination tools for the clairaudient, such as rustling leaves, water tumbling, waves crashing, grasses sighing in the wind, even rain on the roof.

The empath is also known as one who is clairsentient, or "clear feeling." They can feel the emotional energy from people or places. They may even sense a person's energy from an object that they once possessed. Empaths tend to be sensitive souls who avoid confrontational situations. They can learn to protect themselves from overloading through various exercises and magical techniques, without lessening their ability. Can you instantly read a room when you walk in? Do large crowds or being surrounded closely by strangers on the subway or at a concert make you feel a little distressed or uncomfortable? Is going to weddings and funerals (highly emotional events), even of people you barely know or have never even met, very difficult for you? If so, you might be an empath.

Empaths are drawn to divination methods that allow the emotions to come into play, sometimes through physical contact, such as palm reading. They also tend to have an ability to read people's auras.

There is also the intuitive, someone who just "knows" certain things in certain situations. It's literally a gut feeling: you feel it in your solar plexus if something is right or wrong. Are you confident and tend to leap before you look? Have you had a sinking feeling upon meeting someone or coming into a certain situation? Do you know how people are going to act before they do? Have you made a choice, such as taking a different route home from work, only to find out that something bad happened on your regular route? Do you follow your instincts? If so, you might be an intuitive.

Intuitives are drawn to divination methods that allow them to trust their gut. Water witching, pendulums, and other forms of divining (through forked twigs, copper rods, etc.) are all good choices for intuitives. They also may use any other form of divination, but they tend to go with what they feel rather than what an oracle deck instruction book tells them each card means. Most people who read the tarot tap into this ability in some form or another in addition to the classical card meanings.

Many people are a combination of all the above different kinds of witchy psychic skills. I am a clairvoyant with precognitive dreams and am also highly empathic. I have learned over the years to trust in my intuition, and with the work that I have done and continue to do on my psychic skills, I am bringing my intuitive skills up to the mark. I also sometimes hear the voice of the divine, especially after meditation, and so am brushing up on my clairaudient skills. For a great book on how to develop these skills, I highly recommend Ellen Dugan's *Natural Witchery: Intuitive, Personal & Practical Magick*.

Once you have determined your natural skills, you can then choose a method of divination that works well for you. Only you will know what works best for you, and don't forget to experiment. You may find that you have a propensity and proficiency somewhere that surprises you!

Methods of Divination

Now it's time to get down to business. What method are you going to use to receive those messages from the divine? It's a personal choice, and it may take some trial and error before you find one that really works for you. I use three different kinds of divination methods in my own hedge witch practice: the Norse runes, the witch's runes, and an oracle card deck. Each of these methods yields different results, so it will really depend not only on the question or information that I am seeking, but also who I am seeking it from. The witch's runes and the oracle card deck that I use are good all-rounders, so I can connect to any of the deities that I work with for their aid in the reading. When I am working with the Norse runes, I usually call upon Freya. This might surprise some because it was Odin who discovered the runes, but I don't have a personal relationship with Odin. I do have a bond with Freya, so I call to her as the Lady of Magic to help me in my work. It was Freya who taught Odin the oracular method of seidr, a trance-divination process, so I like to believe that in return Odin taught Freya how to work with the runes. At any rate, she has helped me in my runework for years, and I'm sticking with it. Freya also aids me on the rare occasion I have performed seidr, but to describe that in further detail would require a whole other book! [54]

You might favour the tarot or the Druidic ogham or any number of divination processes. You might even make your own divinatory set with items from your local environment that have meaning for you. An acorn for possibility, strength, and the masculine. A dried rosebud for love, beauty, and the feminine. A holed stone for the Fair Folk, Witchcraft, and magical workings. A birch twig for new beginnings and inspiration. A hazelnut for wisdom. A small feather for flight, astral travel, freedom—you get the idea. Use what works for you and that has meaning. That is the most important factor in divination.

There are so many different types of oracular work, such as tasseomancy, the art of divining through the tea leaves left over in a cup (*tasse* is the French word for cup), or aeromancy, the art of divining through clouds and other atmospheric phenomena. There is dendromancy, the reading of leaves and branches on trees, or phyllomancy, a way to determine hidden messages through the rustling of said leaves. There is the more well-known astrology or the increasingly more popular bibliomancy, the art of allowing a book to open and reading the first message you see there. There is even stercomancy, the art of divining through seeds left in bird droppings. If it works, it works!

---

54 For an introduction to seidr, see my video on my YouTube channel, Joanna van der Hoeven, and the video "What is Seidr? Heathen on the Heath Series," https://youtu.be/twUFENb0zZg (uploaded August 28, 2021).

It may take some time and a lot of trial and error before you find a method that works for you, and that is perfectly fine. This is going to be a life skill that you will acquire, so it will take some effort to fully materialise. There may be wrong turns taken and lessons learned, which are extremely valuable teachers in their own right. Experiment and see what feels right for you. Look to the deities you work with and see if they have a connection to any particular form of divination or even natural phenomena. If you work with a sea goddess or god, then you might be able to go into a trance through the sound and motion of the waves on a seashore and connect to them in that state in order to divine.

Hedge riding in and of itself can be a tool for divining. When we cross the hedge over and into the otherworld, we can do so with the intention of finding the answers that we are seeking. Things we may come across in our hedge riding can be read, and the symbols interpreted in much the same way as a dream might (which is called oneiromancy, just so you know). You can perform this on the astral plane or in the physical world with a walk in an area that you feel is right for the work. I have gone to the heathland where I live on many occasions to do a hedge riding and see what messages appear as I move physically through the landscape (see my previous book, *The Path of the Hedge Witch,* for an example of how to do this).

Divination is not only a practice that is used to ascertain information about our own lives, however. Divination can also help us better understand our own locality and environment. Divining, water witching, dowsing, and doodlebugging are all names for a method that helps you find underground water in a certain area, usually using a forked tree branch but also sometimes using a pendulum or copper rods. These tools can also help one find energy or ley lines in a landscape, which can be tapped into for your own magic or which can be fed energy in reciprocity. You can search for any number of phenomena using these methods: lost property, treasure, minerals, even oil (but let's refrain from those fossil fuels, please). I have used copper rods to find paths and lines of energy both in my home and in the landscape. When a source or line of energy is encountered, the rods will suddenly cross over each other. These are a fun and inexpensive way of working a little magic in your local area and are small enough to be carried in your purse, handbag, or backpack, which is always a bonus.

Intuition and Discernment

A final few words in this chapter on using your intuition and also increasing your ability for discernment. Intuition should always, *always* be used with common sense. What we think might be intuition may, in fact, be wishful thinking. It is important to use our discernment to distinguish between what it is that we want to happen and what is actually going to happen. If you are using your instincts and intuition, you will usually feel it in your solar plexus area, sometimes as a slight tug, say, to indicate that you should take this road instead of that one or talk to this person instead of that one. Our eyes can deceive us, as can our other senses when we are not using them clearly. The "clear" in clear sight, sound, etc. is all-important. We must ensure that we are using our psychic abilities clearly and not muddy the waters with wish fulfilment, glamour, or even fear. We can think we are using our intuition to avoid a meeting at work, when really we just don't want to be called upon to do a presentation, make a suggestion, or even offer our opinion. We could let our fear get in the way of our lives and hide it behind intuition. Discerning between fear, wishes, and false hopes will help us greatly improve our psychic skills. Meditation will most definitely help in this area.

First and foremost, be sensible in your choices. You don't have to close yourself down to the magic all around you in order to be grounded and practical. But at the same time, don't think that everything is a premonition or a message from the gods. Sometimes a black cat crossing your path means that it's feeding time at your neighbour's three doors down. Sometimes a hunch that we have about someone or something doesn't come to pass or you may have totally misread a situation. Not every dream is precognisant: sometimes it's just that pizza you wolfed down at 11 p.m. when you got home from the show.

With time and experience, you will know the real forms of divination, the proper messages from the divine, from the other messages that you may be receiving or think you are receiving. Remember, once again, that this is a skill you develop. You may have a natural propensity for a certain form of divination, but that doesn't mean you're going to get it right all the time without a little practice. Trust your intuition, for sure, but also work hard at developing the skills you have.

We never stop learning in our craft.

SUGGESTED READING

The Natural Magician: Practical Techniques for Empowerment by
   Vivianne Crowley (Penguin, 2003)
   This should be on every magical practitioner's bookshelf, in
   my opinion. With examples from the author's own life, it is an
   invaluable source for all witches.

*The Natural Psychic: Ellen Dugan's Personal Guide to the Psychic
   Realm* by Ellen Dugan (Llewellyn, 2015)
   Another work by Ellen Dugan, again exploring aspects of psychic
   work in an easygoing writing style.

Natural Witchery: Intuitive, Personal & Practical Magick by Ellen
   Dugan (Llewellyn, 2019)
   Everything you wanted to know about how to develop your psychic
   skills.

I'm about to do a rune reading for someone. I set out the cloth that I created for rune reading, which is a piece of white cotton that I hand-painted with a symbol for the element of earth, an equal-armed cross within a circle, and on either side a fallow deer stag and hind (my fylgjur). I know that these empower my work, lending their aid to my readings. I take a moment and settle in front of the cloth, sitting with my eyes closed and slowing down my breath.

I ground and centre myself using the roots and branches meditation. I then call out to Freya, connecting to her energy, and ask her to aid me in my work. I can feel her golden light within my heart, expanding outwards and into the room. She is with me, and I am ready to begin.

I pick up the bag of runes and pour them out into my hand. I place the bag down and cup the runes now in both hands, bringing them up to my forehead. "Freya, help me find what it is that they need to know," I ask, and I blow a gentle breath over the runes. I then close my hands together and hold them about a foot above the cloth. I open my hands and let the runes fall.

Some land within the circle, some just outside, some off the cloth completely. Those that are facedown are left out of the reading. Those off the cloth but still right-side up are showing distant influencing energies. Those on the cloth but outside the circle are showing influencing energies that are much closer to home. And those runes right-side up that lie within the circle are the direct runes that pertain to the reading. Depending on where they fall in the circle is when things will happen, have happened, or indeed are happening in this moment.

I gaze over the runes and take them all in, getting a general feel for the reading before I dive deep into each rune. I then pick up my notebook and write down, rune by rune, the reading for the person, interpreting each one according to their traditional meanings, their placement on the cloth, and their placement near other runes, as well as using my intuition.

When I am done, I will email the person with the results. I have been working with them for many months now, and each reading is flowing into the previous one beautifully. It's wonderful and an honour to witness someone's spiritual progress.

I thank Freya for aiding me in my rite. I scoop up the runes, put them safely away in their bag, and neatly fold up the cloth until next time. I ground myself once more before I get up and get on with the rest of the day's tasks. I will leave an offering for Freya during my nightly meditation session.

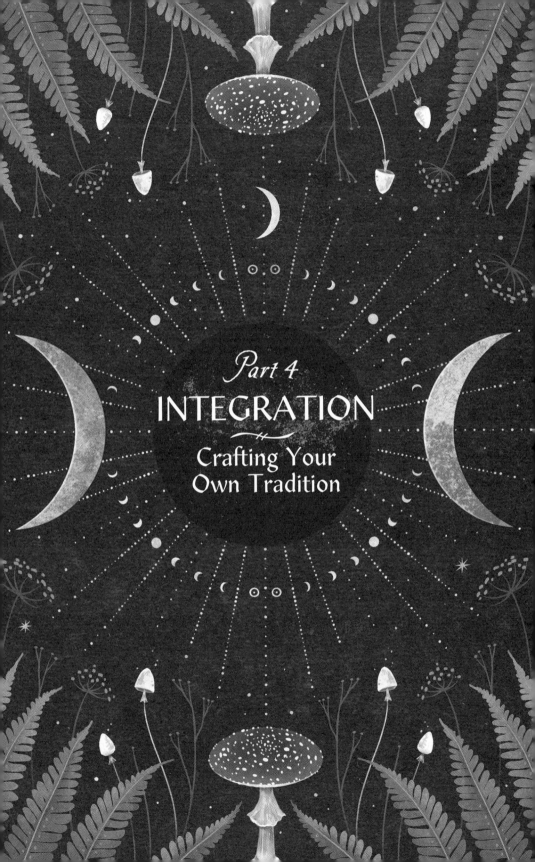

Part 4

INTEGRATION

Crafting Your
Own Tradition

Chapter 12

Integrating the Cycles of the Seasons

They broke my heart and they killed me,
but I wouldn't die. They tried to bury
me; they didn't realise I was a seed.

• • • • • •

Sinéad O'Connor[55]

In my previous book, I introduced you to the solar path, the eight festivals on the Wheel of the Year, or sabbats, as they are known. I provided some background information for each, as well as some ideas for each sabbat. In that work, I also described circle casting and other information the hedge witch can use in their rituals, so I will not go over the basic information here on how to cast the circle, call in the elements, invoke deity, and so forth.

In this chapter, I will provide you with a full set of simple rituals that you can use to celebrate the turning of the seasons. These rituals are not complicated and can be performed with minimum fuss. They will usually run around a half hour in total, but you can make them longer if you so

---

55   "Sinead O'Connor wanted to be remembered as a 'seed' that would live forever," Female First, www.femalefirst.co.uk/celebrity/sinead-oconnor-wanted-remembered -seed-live-forever-1383612.html (August 13, 2023).

desire. Use them as they are or adapt them or even use them as inspiration for your own rituals.

Celebrate the never-ending cycle of life, death, and rebirth through these rituals. Keeping them close to your heart will align you to the natural ebb and flow of the energy of the land. Wherever you live, take your inspiration first and foremost from the land itself. It is here where you will truly begin to integrate into the natural flow of the seasons and their energy. Get to feel the cycles of the natural world around you, which also flow through you, as you too are a part of it, a contributing member of an ecosystem.

The rituals below are based on the land where I live in Suffolk, England. If you live in the antipodes, then you may feel more comfortable reversing the sabbats and celebrate Yule in your wintertime, which would be summer in England. Do what feels right for you and for the land where you live.

Yule

On the Winter Solstice, on or around December 21, Witches and folks from other Pagan traditions gather to celebrate the return of the sun, welcoming the growing light of each day. The circle and altar may be decorated with holly, ivy, mistletoe, and evergreens. The colours for this holiday are red and green. Have a white candle nearby to light at dawn.

For this ritual, you may want to do an all-night vigil. Turn off the indoor lights and central heating if you wish to show your courage throughout the longest night.

Set up the altar, light any candles and incense you wish to use, and prepare yourself for the ritual by grounding and centring. Cast the magic circle. Invoke the elements. Call to the Goddess. Call to the God.

Stand before the altar and say these or similar words:

> On this, the longest night, we give thanks
> to the earth, to the Goddess
> and welcome the Lord of Light with the return of the sun.
> As the days will slowly brighten, so too do our hearts lighten.
> In honour of the longest night, we put out all fires
> to show our courage in the coming year.

The Wild Hunt rides—Herne in the night
skies; the Hunter we honour too.
When the sun stands still, we wait until
the lengthening light brings a dawn new.

Blow out all candles and remain in the darkness. Then say:

From out of darkness, there is light.
From death, there is rebirth.
From out of fear, courage to see the day.

(To be repeated at dawn.)

Sit and think of the Wheel of the Year, contemplating the cycle of life. Pass the seasons through your mind and know that they speak to your heart and soul. Review how your year went and how you can make improvements for the following year.

Welcome the time of greatest darkness and the soon-to-be lengthening days. Thank the earth and the Goddess for her bounty. Honour the quietude and darkness of the longest night with a silent meditation. Leave an offering of food and drink, then close down the circle. Remain in your vigil throughout the night, if you desire, but if that's not possible, don't worry: simply get up just before sunrise, if you are able, for the next part of this ritual.

At dawn, take the white candle and light it, saying the above chant as the sun appears over the horizon. If a fireplace is nearby, light the Yule log and celebrate in its warmth.

Imbolc

On January 31 through February 1, witches celebrate Imbolc. Some celebrate Candlemas on February 2, but this is a reflection of the Christian version of Imbolc. Imbolc is associated with new growth, as seeds begin to germinate beneath the winter frost and snow. It is a popular initiatory period, so if you wish to begin a new endeavour in your Hedge Witchcraft or dedicate yourself to the gods or your own path, then Imbolc is a good time. Its colours are white and green.

Have some seeds and a pot of rich soil for this ritual. Set up the altar, light any candles and incense you wish to use, and prepare yourself for the ritual by grounding and centring. Cast the magic circle. Invoke the elements. Call to the Goddess. Call to the God.

Stand before the altar and say the following:

> On this day/night we give thanks to the Goddess
> and honour the God's growing light.
> As the seeds sprout in the warming earth, so too do our
> hopes for the coming year come into manifestation.
> To show appreciation for the cycle of life,
> the seed is planted, the candles are lit
> on this night of Imbolc, the season of hope.

Chant:

> The candles are lit, the fire is glowing
> The seeds are sprouting, the magic is growing

Take a moment to feel the energy of this time—of newfound hopes fed by older memories. Take the seeds that you have chosen and plant them now in the pot of soil. Chant the above words over the plant, blessing it with your love. If you so desire, you may put a hope or wish into the seed, having it manifest when the plant grows to maturity. Write down that wish on a piece of paper and push it into the soil of the pot. The wish will grow as the seeds sprout and come into fruition if you tend to it on both the physical plane as well as magically. Depending on the seeds you choose, this could either take a short while (watercress, for example, or grass seeds) or they might come to fruition much later. Close down your ritual as appropriate.

Take good care of the seeds as they sprout and grow to maturity, and your magic will correspond to your work.

Spring Equinox

Around March 21 the Spring Equinox arrives and is welcomed into our lives. On that special day, the hours of daylight and nighttime are equal, soon to be tipping into longer days than nights, even as the buds are opening on the trees. The sap is flowing and the energy is growing as the days become warmer.

Prepare an eggshell or several, if you so desire, by blowing out the yolk: prick the bottom and top with a pin, then gently but firmly blow the albumen and yolk out through the bottom (use it for breakfast afterwards). Have some paints handy for this ritual. You can also make papier-mâché eggs if you are vegan.

Set up the altar, light any candles and incense you wish to use, and prepare yourself for the ritual by grounding and centring. Cast the magic circle. Invoke the elements. Call to the Goddess. Call to the God.

Stand before the altar and say the following:

On this night we give thanks to the Goddess
and celebrate with the God in his youthful joy.
As the days become warmer with the promise of summer,
so too do our hearts warm to the coming light.
The Green Man is stirring in the countryside
and our hearts are stirring with him.
All nature is preparing for fertility
by shrugging off the long winter's sleep.
So too do we cast off the confines of
winter and celebrate spring.

Chant:

The buds are swelling, the sap is flowing
The cold abates, the sun is growing

Now dance, if you so wish! Feel the earth waking up beneath your feet. Clap your hands and make some noise. Get out the drums and rattles and awaken the earth from its slumber. Chant or sing the above as you do so, and wake up your own soul in likeness.

Once the dance is complete, sit and calm the mind and body both. Then take up your eggshell and think of the coming fertility in nature as you paint it in any way you choose. Wrap some cotton or other natural fibre threads around the egg to hold it and cradle it for hanging, or use a natural glue to stick a thread to the top. Enchant the finished product with a wish or desire, then close down the ritual. Go outside and hang the eggshell in a tree. Bless the eggshell and the tree as you tie it on, and say a prayer for the goddess of the earth. If you don't have access to a garden, bring some branches into your home, place them in a vase, and hang eggs among them to decorate your home with springtide joy.

Beltane

From sunset on April 30 to sunset on May 1 is Beltane, the time when the land blossoms in full fertility. It is the start of summer here in the east of England. This is a time for joyous celebration, as the trees are out in full leaf. Gather some of the first summer flowers in honour of the Lord and Lady.

Have to hand three ribbons of pleasing colours, as well as a candle or even a fire if you are so lucky, preferably outdoors. Set up the altar, decorate with flowers, light any candles and incense you wish to use, and prepare yourself for the ritual by grounding and centring. Cast the magic circle. Invoke the elements. Call to the Goddess. Call to the God.

Stand before the altar and say the following:

> On this night we give thanks to the Goddess and feel the
> strength of the God as he unites his energy with her.
> From their joyous union life springs forth,
> and all nature dances to their song.
> The fire of life shines bright in the night
> as all gather to celebrate their union.
> Hail to the Earth! Hail to the Green Man!

Chant:

> The circle is cast, the fire is alight
> as the magic is felt this Beltane night

The chant may be used while scrying in the fire or candle, just before a hedge riding, or when treading the mill. This is a perfect time for trancework of all kinds, especially to connect with the Fair Folk. Make full use of this special time.

When you've returned from your work, take the three ribbons you previously selected and braid them together, repeating the chant once again. Bind what you have learned in your hedge witch's path into the ribbons. Weave the union of the Goddess and God into the work too, uniting two energies to create a third. You can use this ribbon in future trancework to give your hedge riding an extra boost.

The circle is then closed down. An old countryside tradition for May Day here in the UK is for women to go outside at dawn and bathe face and hands in the morning dew to promote beauty; I'm sure in these modern times anyone is welcome to this tradition. Dancing in the dew is also fun, and by doing so you can create your own faerie circle on the ground. Gather up a few more of the first summer flowers, leaving an offering to the plants. Have them decorate the home and let their energies suffuse it with love.

Litha

The Summer Solstice, around June 21, is a time of great magic. It is also the longest day, when the God as the Green Man is at his full strength. It is a magical time—a time when the Fair Folk walk the land. Collect some fresh herbs from the wild and have to hand. Build a fire or have a lit charcoal disc that you can safely burn the herbs upon. A balefire is traditional at this time of year, created of nine woods: alder, ash, birch, hawthorn, hazel, holly, oak, rowan, and willow. A candle will do for those who don't have access to a fire.

Set up the altar, light any candles and incense you wish to use, and prepare yourself for the ritual by grounding and centring. Cast the magic circle. Invoke the elements. Call to the Goddess. Call to the God.

Stand before the altar and say the following:

> On this night we give thanks to the Goddess
> and honour the God at his full strength.

The earth is alive with the height of the season
and we celebrate with nature what they have given us.
The Green Man is at the height of his
power, pulsing through the land.
The boundaries between the worlds are thin
and we open our hearts and minds to the land.

Chant:

On this night when magic is all around
the boundary of Faery can be found.
Listen close and listen long
and you will hear the faeries' song.

Perform a hedge riding if you will or simply meditate and listen for the faeries' song. You might feel a humming coming from the earth itself or the sound of music or bells on the breeze. Open yourself to it, and welcome the magic into your life.

Afterwards, take the herbs that you have collected and offer them to the Fair Folk by throwing them into the fire, transforming them into the smoke of spirit.

Midsummer is also a classic time for magic, and any worked this night will have more strength and power. Perform any spellcraft at this time.

The circle is then released. If it is possible, spend this night outdoors. Feel and connect with nature, and enjoy the magic of the night. Listen to the night sounds, look at the stars and moonlight through the trees or upon a windswept hilltop. If your fairy familiar has not made itself known to you, now may be the ideal time to discover them.

Lammas

Held at the first harvest of wheat or barley, or July 31 to August 1 if going by the calendar, this celebration is a precursor to the other harvest festivals to come. Here in East Anglia, it denotes the start of harvest season, which differs from summer in the energetic feel: the growing time is over, and now it is the time of reaping. The cereal plants are drooping their heavy heads even as the sun shines hot and bright. Some of the young animals of spring are nearing maturity, and some of spring's hopes are now fulfilled. For the ritual, have some home-baked bread and other seasonal foods.

Set up the altar, light any candles and incense you wish to use, and prepare yourself for the ritual by grounding and centring. Cast the magic circle. Invoke the elements. Call to the Goddess. Call to the God.

Stand before the altar and say the following:

> On this night we give thanks to the Goddess
> and honour the God for his rewarding light.
> The seeds are falling; the sun is warming
> all life with the song of summer.
> Our hopes of the spring are coming to pass
> and we share in the bounty that is given to us.
> Hail to the Green Man for the green and growing things.
> Hail to the earth and the bounty that she brings.

Chant:

> Seeds fall as the corn stands high
> We break the bread and hold cups high
> In this time of harvest gathered round
> We celebrate the bounty of sky and ground

Take the fresh bread and break it with your hands, savouring the feel and smell. Taste it and thank the Goddess and God for their bounty. Hold the cup high (beer is ideal for this ritual, to honour the barley harvest) and do the same. Leave a good portion as an offering, and place it outside upon the ground. For those living in cities, you may simply pour it out down the drain after the ritual. You may like to say a chant to make this special, such as "From the river to the sea, an honoured gift from me.")

The circle is then released. Corn dollies are traditional at this time of year, so try to find some to decorate the home and altar—or, better yet, have a go at making your own. Ornamental corn is also festive and decorative, and it may be found in a wide variety of colours to create a seasonal decoration for the first harvest.

Autumn Equinox

Around September 21 is the Autumn Equinox, the second of the three harvest sabbats. The crops are still being taken in, the hedgerows full of bounty. The days are becoming noticeably shorter, and the air is turning chill. The leaves are changing as nature prepares for the long winter months. On the equinox itself, the hours of daylight and night are equal once again before falling into the longer, darker time of winter.

Gather in a basket some fallen leaves, acorns, and berries for the following ritual. Have also a substantial offering to give: local, seasonal food is ideal. Set up the altar, light any candles and incense you wish to use, and prepare yourself for the ritual by grounding and centring. Cast the magic circle. Invoke the elements. Call to the Goddess. Call to the God.

Stand before the altar and say the following:

> On this night we give thanks to the Goddess
> and God for all their abundance.
> As the crops and feasts show what the planting has done
> so too have our hopes for the year come and gone.
> We reap the rewards through darkness and light
> and prepare ourselves for the long winter night.
> The Green Man fades into the nights and
> Herne the Hunter soon rides the heights.

Chant:

> The crops are gathered, the second harvest done
> We celebrate the fullness of all we have won
> We reap the seeds we have sown in the year
> And honour the land with good heart and cheer

Take up the basket of leaves, nuts, and berries and scatter its contents around the circle while reciting the above chant. Afterwards, contemplate the cycle of life, the budding of the leaves that are now changing and will bloom once again. Meditate upon the balance of darkness and light, of the equal day and night. See how that is reflected in your life as well as in nature. When you are ready, give your offering back to nature: a gift for a gift, a spiritual exchange. Say these or similar words:

> From the gods to the earth to us
> From us to the earth to the gods
> I offer this in reciprocity
> And give my blessings to the land
> Farewell to the Green Man!

The circle is released. The food offerings may be buried or left out for the local wildlife if appropriate. If you are unable to leave an offering outside, dispose of it in your compost or however you are able to dispose of foodstuffs. You may like to make it a bit more special when placing it in the bin by saying something like "A gift for a gift from me; love, honour, and blessed be." If you have an apple tree or an orchard nearby, now is the ideal time for picking those beautiful gifts. Try your hand at baking apple pies, crumbles, sauces, or even homemade cider. Infuse the food with your love, and always leave some as an offering.

Samhain

October 31 is where we say farewell to the solar aspect of the God until the light is reborn at Yule. Only when we see the green returning to the land do we know that Herne the Hunter no longer rides the Wild Hunt from the otherworld and the land of the dead but instead comes back to us as the Green Man. For the next few months, the God will act in his role as psychopomp, aiding the souls of the dead to their realms beyond the veil. We honour him in this aspect, even as we honour him in his other guises, for without death there can be no life; without darkness there cannot be light.

Samhain is also a time to reflect upon the past year and honour the ancestors who have gone before. It is a time also to meditate upon our place in the wheel of life, death, and rebirth.

Have an apple and a symbol of the Wheel of the Year upon the altar, if possible, or a pentacle plate. Set up the altar, light any candles and incense you wish to use, and prepare yourself through grounding and centring. If working indoors, have some fire on the altar, such as a candle or in the hearth. If outside, you can have a firepit, a circle surrounded with candles in lanterns, or even torches for extra dramatic flair.

Cast the magic circle. Invoke the elements. Call to the Goddess. Call to the God. Stand before the altar and say the following:

On this night we give thanks to the Goddess
at the third and final harvest.
Farewell, Lord of Light; may you be reborn soon.
I now honour the Lord of Shadows, Herne the Hunter,
and the Wild Hunt as it rides the night skies.

Chant:

The wheel is turning
The Samhain fire is burning

Repeat; use as a trance chant for hedge riding or treading the mill, should you so wish.

Afterwards, take the apple and cut it open sideways through the core, revealing the pentagram within. Place the two halves upon the Wheel of the Year or the pentacle. Look upon the two halves, each with the pentacle in the centre, and see them as the light and the dark, the day and the night, the polarity of forces that contains everything in between them. The Green Man is now Herne the Hunter, and yet they are one and the same. Meditate upon this before giving up the apple as an offering.

Then take a moment to honour the ancestors with prayers and thanks or in silent meditation. Light a candle for them that will burn throughout the night. This candle should be placed in the window of the home or by the front door to light the way for the departed souls on their way to the Summerland. An offering of a meal left outside to sustain them on their long journey is also traditional.

Close down the ritual, ground and centre, and spend a few moments in the darkness, welcoming it into your life for the next few months.

• • •

I hope that this set of simple rituals inspires you in your own hedge witch path. May the seasons bless you with their energy and wisdom.

Suggested Reading

In the Circle: Crafting the Witches' Path by Elen Hawke (Llewellyn, 2000)

An out-of-print text but one that provides a beautifully crafted tradition of working with the seasons.

The Magical Year: Seasonal Celebrations to Honour Nature's Ever-Turning Wheel by Danu Forest (Watkins, 2016)

A British wisewoman's guide to working through the Wheel of the Year. A brilliant work.

Seasons of Witchery: Celebrating the Sabbats with the Garden Witch by Ellen Dugan (Llewellyn, 2018)

Ellen Dugan's first works were about her as the Garden Witch, and this work continues in that theme, along with ideas for magically decorating the home and more.

Witch's Wheel of the Year: Rituals for Circles, Solitaries and Covens by Jason Mankey (Llewellyn, 2019)

A huge work that should be on everyone's reading list, this is a text that is well-researched and well-written.

It is Lammas, and the combine harvesters are a dull roar in the background. I walk to a nearby field that has just been harvested. The week before, the wheat was drooping their heads, ready to be cut down and transformed into sustenance. The red poppies dotted themselves throughout the rows of wheat, taking up any space that they could. They are symbolic of the blood on the plough, the blood of the small animals that don't get away in time during the reaping of the harvest. They are the blood of John Barleycorn, cut down and thrashed and transformed into bread and beer. They remind us that in life there is death, and in death there is life.

I had prayed the week before that when this field was harvested, it would be done with the little creatures in mind. Too many farmers spiral their machines inwards, leaving nowhere for the animals to run and hide until they are cut down with the last of the wheat in the centre of the field. If the field is instead harvested from one side to the other, it gives the little ones a chance to run into the next field or hedgerow and find another home.

As I ran my hands across the bowed heads of the wheat, the sun beating down upon us, I opened myself to one of the great mysteries of this path. I felt it deep in my core. It was not just a thought, an abstract, but something that I felt in my heart and soul. A tear escaped my eye as I felt this great gift, and I said my thanks softly as the breeze began to blow, the wheat sheaves dancing in response.

Now the field is but stubble, and the bareness of it is stark and harsh. I give my offering of fresh-baked bread and beer, leaving it in a corner of the field. This small corner is full of wildflowers, a little wilderness right next to the stark rows of stubble and cracked, parched soil exposed now to the sun. This little patch left in a field is known locally as the Devil's Plantation, a small part left aside for the spirits of nature. It is here where I feel called to leave the offering, in this liminal space between the wild and the tilled soil, on the edges of life and death.

Chapter 13

Integrating the Cycles of the Moon

Be both soft and wild. Just like the
Moon. Or the storm. Or the sea.

• • • • • •

Victoria Erickson

In this chapter, I will provide you with a full lunar set of rituals for an entire year, inspired by my local landscape and from which you can either work directly or adapt and change to suit your location and needs. This is not holy writ; rather, it's inspiration for you to find your own set of lunar rituals for your own practice. Some of the names I give below are traditional, as they resonate with the landscape in which I live, but others are my own names that I have given to better reflect what is happening in nature around me at that particular time.

You may experience a similar climate where you live or have something totally different. Find inspiration in the rituals below to develop something that is meaningful to you and your environment. I have also provided suggestions for a blue moon ritual as well as a black moon ritual.

Cold Moon

The January full moon usually lives up to its name. If there was a midwinter thaw, it's usually gone by now, and we can only dream of warmer days and nights. The next couple of moons are usually the coldest; however, they light up the long nights with their brilliant silvery light and are an absolute joy to behold when one is wrapped up warmly.

This is the first moon of the new year, so we can take some time to reflect and also plan for the year to come. We'll use the energy of this moon to help us achieve our goals, and state our intentions not only for what we wish to accomplish, but also how we can give back for what we have received. It is also a good time to re-dedicate yourself to your path, and we'll incorporate that into this ritual.

In the days leading up to this ritual, write down what you wish to gain from your spiritual practice. Take some time to really think about this, and try to be specific about the year ahead. Broad, general ideas are much harder to accomplish than specific goals. Once you have finalised this, write it out as beautifully as you can on a fresh piece of paper and pour your energy and intention into it, seeing yourself achieving or having already achieved your desire. You can also pour this energy into an object, such as a stone or a piece of artwork that represents your intention.

As well, take some time before this full moon ritual to write down what it is that you feel you are able to give back to your spirituality. This might be in the form of community work, making regular offerings, reaching out to others, cleaning up litter in your local patch, or becoming more involved in your tradition in however you feel you are able. Once this has been defined (and be specific!), write this out too on a fresh piece of paper and infuse it with your intention and energy (or use another object as above, if you are unable to write). Keep the old papers or objects to remind you throughout the year.

Finally, before the ritual, write down or come up with some dedication vows that you will make to your path, the deities, ancestors, Fair Folk—whomever you choose. Make these as simple or as flowery and poetic as you like. Memorise them to recite during your full moon ceremony.

On the night of the cold moon, have a candle or a fire in your space, if you are able. Cast your circle and invoke with your usual method. Once you are ready, hold the piece of paper that stated what you wish to gain from your spiritual practice (or the object, if using one). Visualise: see yourself as having achieved this, and allow the light of the full moon to shine onto the paper, infusing it with lunar power. When ready, light the piece of paper with the candle or fire. Let it burn, throwing it into a heat-proof container or into the fire. See the energy flowing outwards, manifesting your desire. Do the same with the second piece of paper, which contained what you can give back. If you are unable to burn anything, let the lunar light soak into the paper or object and then bury it in the ground as soon as you can.

Take a moment now and simply breathe, attuning yourself to the lunar energies. Breathe them in, letting them fill your body and soul with this mysterious, enchanting light. Let it awaken the joy you felt when you first started out on this path. With this joy, recite your dedication or rededication vows, with the moon and night sky as witness, the Goddess and God within and around you, and the ancestors, Fair Folk, and spirits of place to guide you. Pay attention to any messages that may come from the natural world after you have spoken aloud your words. Do a hedge riding if you so desire.

Finally, pause, soak up this magical time, and then close down the ritual. Celebrate in some special way.

White Lady Moon

The full moon of February often coincides with the first blossoming of the blackthorn tree, although in some years this can be much later. As well, the snowdrops, these beautiful little heralds of spring, are out and carpeting the woods. The days are growing longer, and during this moon we really start to notice the changes from the winter tide to the spring tide.

This is a time to connect with the divine feminine energies in whatever form you choose. The Lady is awakening from her winter slumber, and her energy is now rising. This energy can be seen as serpent energy, like the ley lines that run through the earth, stirring and retreating, moving upwards or back into the earth in correlation with the seasons. Now in the Northern Hemisphere the energy is moving upwards, rising from the earth to meet the warming sun overhead. We celebrate the life-giving energy of the Lady, she who is the tapestry that all life is woven upon, she who is the cycle itself.

The dreams of winter will soon come into manifestation, but these dreams must be kept safe. In this full moon ritual, we will use the energies of the White Lady Moon for purification and protection in the year to come.

Have a large bowl of water to hand for this ritual. Use some moon water (water that has been infused with the light of the full moon) mixed in with the water from your tap; if you have gathered water from a nearby spring, this too will be excellent for this ritual. Essentially, water from your local area is ideal. If you can, gather a blossom or a small branch of the flowering blackthorn, with the tree's permission.

Create sacred space and call in the Goddess. Hold the blossom or the branch in your hand over the bowl (don't worry if you don't have a branch; this ritual will work fine without it). If you live in an area where there is snow, you can substitute the water for a bowl of snow.

Then say the following or something similar:

Lady of the Moon
White Lady of the Spring
Protect my dreams for the year
And offer me your blessing
Lady of the thorn
Silver light upon the tree
Purify my mind, body, and soul
So that I am one with thee

Sprinkle the blossom in the water or stir the branch in the water deosil (clockwise) nine times. If you don't have any blackthorn, simply use your hand to stir nine times. Lift the bowl up to the moon, if visible, and catch its light on the water (or snow). Feel it suffusing with the lunar energies of this season, combining with the blackthorn. Then place the bowl down and anoint yourself with the water (or snow). You may anoint your forehead, lips, heart, solar plexus, and feet. You might like to say something as you do this, such as:

Lady, bless my thoughts, protect my dreams
Lady, bless my words
Lady, bless and protect my heart
Lady, bless my power
Lady, bless and protect me on my path

Think on the year to come, and know that you have been blessed by the Lady. Meditate, then give an offering to the Lady.

Sap Rising Moon

In March the buds are showing on the birch and beech trees, and some early hawthorns are beginning to leaf. Yellow daffodils and forsythia are blooming, opening up to the sun and holding themselves closed to night frosts. Crocuses shine in the garden in the spring sunlight. The earth's energy is humming louder now, waking up—can you feel it? The songs of the birds are louder, the wind speaks of change, and the sun is moving ever toward the northern quarters of the horizon with each and every day. Soon the clocks will change, and the daylight hours will triumph over the darkness.

At this time of the year we are so thankful for the longer days. The winter is always hard, with so little sunlight. The earth is warming to the solar rays, and the ground is soft from the rains. We see the light of spring and rejoice in it. We honour the winter darkness for all that it has taught us even as we turn our faces to the sun just as the flowers do in the spring. If where you live you are still under snow, you can still turn your face toward the sun and give thanks for the longer days.

For this ritual, you will need hard-boiled eggs (make some papier-mâché ones if vegan), paints, and markers or colouring pencils to decorate the eggs. Yes, we are using eggs again, as we did for the Spring Equinox, but here we are using a different magical technique by working with the power of the full moon and burying the eggs in the earth. The time of the full moon will affect what it is that you want with a different energy, so take some time to think about what would work best with the full moon's energies and the earth energies that will affect this work.

First, take a moment to think about what it is that you want to manifest in your life right now. What are your hopes and dreams for this year that you've nurtured through the long winter months? What would you like to bring into your life? How can the full moon's energy work with this goal? After you have decided, take up an egg and begin painting or drawing on it symbols of what it is that you wish to embrace in your life. Use a new egg for each desire, if you have multiple ones. Suggestions are health, healing, love and self-love, acceptance, patience, compassion, endurance, integrity, laughter, fertility, a new job, or new beginnings of any kind. You can do this indoors before the ritual or outside under the light of the moon either before or during your ritual; the timing doesn't matter. Once you are happy with your egg or eggs, create your sacred space, if you haven't done so already, and honour the deities. You might wish to call upon the Goddess of Spring for this rite, the Lady of the Greening who walks with twisted staff, the hosts of Faery following, bringing life unto the land.

Hold up your egg/s (use a basket or bowl if you have more than two) to the light of the moon. Infuse them with lunar energy and the blessings of the Lady of Spring. Ask her to bless your dreams, your hopes, and your desires. Really feel the energy of the Lady going into your work. When it feels that the eggs are full of energy, give her your utmost thanks. After the ritual, bury the eggs somewhere on your property or by a tree in a wood. You can also put them in a plant pot, cover with earth, and pot up a green and growing plant on top. As the plant grows, so too will your dreams manifest. Take care of the land, your plants, and your dreams, and the Goddess will bless your life.

Storm Moon

This April moon tide has it all: cold winds from the north and east, stormy skies abound, and wonderful sunrises and sunsets. When you can have four seasons in one day, the changeable nature of this time is what we will celebrate.

How often do we stick to what we know? Why is the unknown so scary for us? We are, for the most part, creatures of habit. We like stability. We often view change negatively, but when winter turns into spring, and spring into summer, most of us are very glad for it! How can we be more open to change in our lives, and how can we view it from a different perspective?

The storms of the season reflect the storms in our lives. No one's life is without pain and suffering. There are highs and lows in everyone's journey, much as there are highs and lows in barometric pressure. Highs bring sunshine, and lows often bring clouds and rain. We need the lows in our lives in order to understand and enjoy the highs. We need the storms of spring to bring the crops and vegetation to their full glory. The trees, the forest, our water reservoirs: we all need the replenishing element of water, which often comes from spring's storms. April showers bring May flowers!

Before the ritual, think on the major life changes that have occurred in your life. Some will have been good; others, devastating. What we are looking for in this exercise is to learn from the wisdom gained from the experience of our lives. We are not going to focus solely on the positive or the negative, for we know that we need both light and shadow in our lives in order to be complete. When you have come up with some examples of life changes, turn your attention to what you have learned or gained from that experience.

You will need a large bowl of water for this ritual. Set up your sacred space, and call in the deities, spirits of place, Fair Folk, and ancestors as you will. Now gaze upon the moon, if visible, and think on those major changes that have happened in your life. Know that there are more to come. Allow any emotions to flow through you and wash over you like a spring storm, then allow yourself to become calm and nourished by the experience. Draw light from the moon, if you need to, to replenish any energy. See it flowing from the moon into the bowl of water. Take the wisdom that is offered from your experiences and nurture that for your future. Push that into the moon water, and then either drink it or, if you are more adventurous, throw it up over your head and let it fall back down upon you in a great big splash! (If indoors, you can tip the bowl over your head in the bathtub or shower after the ritual.) Just afterwards, say:

> May all my storms be spring storms
> to bring the nourishment that I need!

Close down the ritual in your usual way. Dry off, change your clothes if you need to, and then celebrate in some way the beauty of change and the storm moon's tides.

Quickening Moon

This May moon is all about the greening of the land. The trees are coming out into full leaf, the scent of blossoms is everywhere, and hay fever season has begun. It's an inspirational time of the year, when all life is exploding into action. The house martins and the cuckoos have returned, and the dawn chorus sings with abandon.

This is the time to let loose and really go for it. What is it that you have always wanted to do, but for some reason haven't done yet? Do the thing. Let the energy of this moon and its cycle guide you toward what you desire. It's an excellent time for starting a new course or learning a new magical technique. Trancework and ecstatic rituals are ideal at this time of year. We can ride the current of energy to new heights never before imagined. Take this opportunity.

This ritual is very simple. At the full moon, set up your ritual space as you normally would. When ready, stand in the light of the moon, if possible, and draw its energy into you. Feel the silvery light igniting your passion and your desire for this new project, idea, practice, etc. Let it awaken you to the possibilities.

While the moon's energy is flowing into you, feel it mingling with your own personal power. Feel that power rising within yourself. Begin the following chant, and chant for as long as it takes to get you into an ecstatic or trancelike feeling:

Moonlight
Moon bright
My will
Come to light

Continue to chant, but this time draw up energy from the earth as the trees and all the green and growing things are doing at this time of year. Feel yourself branching out and coming into full leaf. Feel the lush green of your being, new and ready for the world. Begin to move, simply swaying if that is all that is possible. Allow yourself to go even deeper, feeling your soul come alive even as nature is burgeoning around you. If you have a drum, pick it up and start drumming along to your chant. Move around, dance, chant, and feel the power rising. When you feel the power at its peak, pour all of your will and energy into your intention for three final turns of the chant, and then let it fade as slowly as you need it to.

Make an offering to the Lady of the Greening and Jack in the Green. Take a moment to feel the power moving in the worlds, and start your new endeavour knowing that it is blessed with the energy of this moon tide.

Faery Moon

This June moon is also called midsummer moon in my own tradition. The faeries and midsummer go hand in hand, as this is one of the three "spirit nights" that they walk the land. For those who are in good relationship with them, the faeries can bring blessings and insight. For those who are antagonistic toward them, though, they will know fear from the faeries' wrath.

It is important to be good neighbours; in folk history, often the Fair Folk are called "the good neighbours" to emphasise and sustain this relationship. We must learn how to live with the Fair Folk so that we can all be together in harmony. As we are all tied to the land upon which we live, it only makes sense. We share this space with so many other beings, both seen and unseen. We must remember that at all times.

This ritual is best performed outdoors in a wild and lonely place far from humanity. If this is impossible, prepare a special area indoors and have potted plants all around the circle. Make it as magical as you can. Have some milk and honey (vegan options work fine too) for the offering. If you can, spend all night outside. At least spend an hour in the meditative section of this ritual, wherever you are. Take necessary precautions when working with the Fair Folk.

Open the ritual as you normally would do. Pay special attention to calling the Fair Folk. Make this a heartfelt and beautiful call to them, to join you in your midsummer rite (as long as they are in tune with your intention: make sure they understand this). Always be respectful to them. For example, you might say: "I call to the Fair Folk, those of this land, who walk in harmony and friendship with me."

For the main part of the ritual, find a place where you can sit or stand and really feel and see the land around you; you may have to visualise this in your mind if you are indoors. This may be the place where you will be spending the night, should you so wish: staying out of doors near midsummer is always a great experience. Ensure that you have some water for yourself and an offering for the Fair Folk. Give the offering to the Fair Folk at the start of the main ritual section, a little or long way away from you in case wild animals claim it in the name of the Fair Folk. Then say the following (or something similar) and settle down for the night; it will be a short night, don't forget, as it's midsummer. Cast a circle of protection if you feel it is necessary to do so.

Lord and Lady of the Green
Bright Ones in the Night
I honour you and all your kin
For you set my soul alight
Be with me during this magic tide
I await the Fairy Ride

Spend the time in silence but alert. They may come to you in any type of form, whether it be wild animal, shining light, wind, the sound of bells, the sounds of horses' hooves, music, or even laughter. Honour them without overdoing it, with words either spoken aloud or with feelings emanating from your heart. Listen to any wisdom they have to share. They may choose to continue working with you in the future. Ensure that you say "May there always be friendship between us" at the end of the interaction.

Only you can discover what awaits you on this night.

Barleycorn Moon

July's barley or barleycorn moon is a time of celebration. There is a moment, a break, just before or during the start of the hard work as the harvest season begins. In July we celebrate the joys of summer: the long, warm days and the bounty of our gardens and the land around us. We see the barley, wheat, and rye ripening in the fields, holding the potential and promise of nourishment throughout the year to come, soon to be harvested. We see our own spiritual harvest, taking stock of the seeds of intention that were planted in the spring and have now come to fruition. What worked and what didn't? How can we celebrate the joys while learning from the sorrows? Now is the time to dance, to sing to the spirits of place, and honour the bountiful abundance that summer and the earth have to give.

Decorate a sunwheel with ribbons of yellow, gold, or orange. (A sunwheel is an equal-armed cross inside of a circle.) You can make one from a florist's wreath, which you can find at most craft shops and use again and again. I like to use one that is made of woven branches. Tie to it greenery from your local environment and anything else that appeals to you. Place it in a good spot where you will be able to dance around it. Attach it to a staff, if you like, and either stick the end of the staff into the ground or place it in a bucket of sand so that it stands upright.

Open the ritual and call in the elements, the spirits of place, the ancestors, the Fair Folk, and the gods.

Give an offering in thanks for the beginning or the coming of the harvest season. Praise the earth and the gifts of the Mother; honour the strength and spirit of the grain. Mark this moment in time when the tide of summer is high, even as we begin to see the nights starting to shorten after the Summer Solstice. See the turning of the tide, where the corn ripening in the fields echoes the rhythms of drawing inwards now that the time of the greatest light has passed. Energy is being passed into the seeds to hold the potential for the coming year. And so the cycle continues.

State what you are thankful for during this, the first harvest. Praise your deities and the land. Thank them and dedicate yourself to working with them throughout the cycles of your life. Any event that you are especially grateful for is praised and shown the deepest gratitude.

And now, dance! Put on some of your favourite music, and dance sunwise around the sunwheel. Let the energy of your dance infuse the land with gratitude and joy. Dance for the gods, the land, the spirits, the Fair Folk, and the ancestors. Dance for your own joy and pleasure. If you are unable to dance, then sing, chant, or do whatever you can to express your deepest gratitude for this, the first harvest.

Heather (Ling) Moon

The heather (or ling, as the bell heather is known here in Suffolk) moon is the August moon that falls between the first two harvests. The heather is out in full bloom on the heathland, and the beauty and magic of this hardy plant inspires us even as the hot summer sun beats down upon the sandy soil. This plant is a survivor, thriving in the most difficult of conditions and yet providing nourishment for the bees, butterflies, and other pollinating insects where other plants are unable in the dry, arid soil. This is a moon about persistence, about giving and receiving, about providing for those often neglected, and for providing us with what we personally need to see us through the rest of the harvest season.

The deer are getting ready for the rut in the coming months. The velvet of antlers is being shed and the stags are fattening up. The blackberries are out, the mugwort is high, and the last of the summer sunshine shines down upon all without discretion. The gifts of summer, the beauty of the season, is available to all who have only to open their eyes and see it.

Open the ritual and call in the elements, the spirits of place, the Fair Folk, the ancestors, and the gods.

Have a bowl of heather on the altar. Call down the energy of the moon and direct it into the heather. Put aside some heather blossom to later sprinkle around the boundaries of your home or property and provide abundance, good luck, strength, and protection. Place some of the heather in a small pouch or charm bag, if you wish, to carry with you through the winter months.

If there is anything you need help with from the gods, the spirits of place, etc., then now is the time to ask for it. There is no point in trying and failing on your own. We all need the help of others sometimes, just as the beautiful heather provides nourishment for the insects in the harshest of the heathland conditions. We are all part of this grand thing called life, and we depend on each other to get through it.

Drum, clap, sing, or chant your thanks, and give back some of your energy to the land. Honour the Lady of the Heather and the Lord of the Stags. Sing their praises, wish them well for the season, and offer them your love and blessings.

Harvest Moon

The harvest moon is the height of the harvest season. The second of the three harvest moons, this is the traditional time of gratitude, community, and coming together to celebrate. In September the fields are giving up their bounty; farmers are supremely busy, and the earth is yielding her gifts. In many parts of the world, this is a season where we give thanks for the blessings that we have; it's a chance to give back in reciprocity. It is also a turning point where we near the time of the equinox and see how the energies are shifting in nature, whether it is the leaves changing colour, the birds migrating overhead, or simply a chill in the air that heralds the coming winter.

Gather some fresh apples and have them in a small basket on your altar. Open the ritual and call in the elements, the spirits of place, the ancestors, the Fair Folk, and the gods.

Honour the time and the season. Give thanks for the fresh and local food from your area, and acknowledge all the elements that brought it to bear: the sun, the wind, the rain, the people working the land, the harvesters, the sellers. Think back to your ancestors and what this time of year meant for them. What is harvested now must last through the winter.

Look at your spiritual harvest. What have you learned in the last year? What can you carry forward through the long winter months? What needs to be left behind, to fall like leaves and become a new form of energy?

Take an apple and slice it in half through the middle. See the five-pointed star within, the magic of life, death, and new potential. All the elements have gone into the creation of this apple, much as the pentagram within shows the elements of earth, air, fire, water, and spirit. Acknowledge this with your body and soul, and see those elements reflected within your own self as well. Then pull out the seeds and place before you. Take up each seed and name something that you wish to let go, and one by one either throw the seeds into a fire or put them, with respect, into a compost bin so that they can be transformed into something new. Offer something back to the earth with reverence and thanks.

Hunter's Moon

Most people in the Northern Hemisphere have heard of October's hunter's moon as well as the previous harvest moon. But just what hunt do we mean when we speak of the hunter's moon? It might simply relate to the start of the hunting season, where animals are hunted in forests, fields, and by streams and lakes. However, there is another hunt that is known in Western Paganism, and that is the Wild Hunt.

Whether it is the Norse or Germanic Wild Hunt led by Odin or Woden or by the goddess Holda, or whether it is the Celtic version led by Gwyn ap Nudd, the Wild Hunt begins to ride at this time of year. At the time of Winternights in the Heathen tradition or Samhain in the Celtic tradition, it is when the Wild Hunt rides across the blustery, wintery skies, collecting the souls of the wayward dead and any other poor unknowing, unfortunate soul who happened to be in their path. For many in the Heathen tradition, the Wild Hunt reaches its peak during the Yule or Winter Solstice period.

But in my own tradition, the Wild Hunt begins in October, when the constellation Orion (the Hunter) is clearly seen striding across the night skies.

The hunter's moon is a liminal time when we are transitioning not only from the season of autumn or harvest to winter, but also from one year to another. It is the ending of the year, which is visible in the natural world around us as we see the last of the summer foliage burst into final colour before fading and falling to the ground, providing sustenance for future generations. At these times when we move from one energy to another, it is said that the veil between the worlds is thin, and we can step through, or meet others stepping through, if we dare . . .

This ritual is best performed out of doors under the light of the full hunter's moon. If you can, go to a wild place where you will not be interrupted (at least by humankind). Bring with you what tools you prefer and an offering. Cast a circle in an area of your choice after asking the spirits of place for their permission. Take all necessary precautions, both physical and metaphysical, to be safe. If indoors, try to make the space as magical and mysterious as possible.

Call to the spirits of place, ancestors of your choice, and the deities. Tell them how you honour this special liminal time. Tell them what you have accomplished this year and what you still have to learn. Extinguish any light. Let the light of the hunter's moon flow through you. With the ancestors watching over you, ask for any messages from the spirits of place, deity, ancestors, or the Fair Folk. Then sit still, watch, and listen.

Does the wind pick up? Do you hear the beating of hooves? Can you feel the Hunt around you? Do you dare to stay outside, solid and certain in your own craft, to know what rides the night sky? Do you dare to be a witch, one who rides the hedge? For in the darkness of the wild, you must find your courage and come to know not only what lies around you in nature, but also what lies within.

When you have finished, close down the circle and leave an offering to the Wild Hunt, the Fair Folk, and the ancestors.

Mist Moon

November is the time when the mists creep onto the heathland at the end of the day and linger about in the early morning light. There is something truly magical about mist; it is water that hangs suspended in the air, appearing at dusk and fading shortly after dawn. It is truly a thing of liminality, where sharp definitions and boundaries are left behind, and we must peer into and venture out into the mists in order to perceive something new and exciting.

Like the stories of Avalon, there is much that is hidden in the mists, both in the world and in our souls. If we are brave enough, if we seek to find that which is hidden in the mists, then we shall come to a land where everything we need is provided, where peace and healing are found, and where we can rest our souls.

This is a time of the year that is not a time: an in-between moon time after the fires of Samhain have gone out and before the Yuletide celebrations. This is a time when the Wild Hunt rides, when the veil between the worlds is still thin. Who knows what we will find in the mists? It is only in these places of liminality that we can truly come to an understanding of both this world and the otherworld.

For this ritual, you will need a chalice filled with wine, mead, milk, or water.

When you cast your circle for this rite, envision it as a misty boundary that takes you between the worlds. This is even more powerful if you can do the ritual outside in the actual mists, but that may not be possible for various reasons.

When you have designated this space between the worlds, open up your heart to the moon's energy and the energy of this moontide. Experience what it feels like to truly be between the worlds. What potential lies there, waiting for you to seek it out?

Gather into yourself the energy of the moon in this time and place, and direct it into the liquid that the chalice holds. Pour that energy into it, infusing it with the power of this liminal moontide. When you are done, catch a reflection of the moon in the liquid, if possible, or envision the reflection in the liquid. Feeling the mists around you, call out to the otherworld to show you what it is that you need to know, that which you seek and quest after in your pursuit of knowledge of the self and the natural world. Gaze into the chalice and take note of what appears. This is an excellent time to do a hedge riding.

When you are ready, close down your rite, and carry the knowledge that you have gained from the otherworld into your everyday life. Seek out the liminal places during this moontide, the dawn and dusk, the seashore, midnight, etc. Work with it to truly understand it and quest the potential that lies just beyond our everyday perceptions. Leave offerings at these special places to establish a relationship with them and a sense of reciprocity.

Midwinter Moon

December's midwinter moon is the full moon nearest to the Winter Solstice. On these longest of winter nights, the full moon is a blessing and shines brightly down upon the earth, reminding us that even in the darkest of times, there is a light that can shine to illuminate our souls. This light is the reflected light of the sun, turned magical and silvery through the earth's only natural satellite. It reminds us that even in the darkest depths of winter, there is always a light that shines.

The winter months are also great for viewing the stars, so go outside and spend some time stargazing. At the time of the full moon some stars are dimmed, but there is plenty to see in the night sky. Orion the Hunter is an easily visible constellation, as are Cassiopeia and the Great Bear or the Plough. Mid-December is also the peak of the Geminids meteor shower.

Wrap up warmly and perform this ritual outdoors, if possible.

Cast the circle and light candles at the four quarters, as well as having a central candle. Call to the spirits of place, the ancestors, the Fair Folk, and the Goddess and God. Stand in the centre or in the north of your circle, and say these or similar words:

> I stand here tonight under the light of the
> midwinter moon. And though the night is long
> and the darkness is great, I have no fear.

Move to the eastern candle, lift it up, and say:

> I honour the powers of the light of the east, the rising sun.

Blow out the candle.
Move to the southern candle, lift it up, and say:

> I honour the powers of the light of
> the south, the noonday sun.

Blow out the candle.
Move to the western candle, lift it up, and say:

> I honour the powers of the light of the west, the setting sun.

Blow out the candle.
Move to the northern candle, lift it up, and say:

> I honour the powers of the light of the
> north, the aurora borealis.

Blow out the candle.
Pick up the central candle and say:

> I honour the flame of my soul, which is eternal.

Blow out the candle.

Spend some time in the darkness, under the light of the moon, if it is visible. Feel its cool light filling and replenishing the light of your own soul. If the moon is not visible, let the darkness envelop your soul, knowing that the spark of eternity shines still within your heart like the light of the distant stars. For you too are made of star stuff, and the magic of the ages flows through you. Feel the blessings of the Goddess flow into you, you who have greeted her at this magical time of the year. Say these or similar words:

Lady of Winter, of the frost and snows
Shining through the bare-branched trees
Illuminating all with its magical glow
Kindle the sacred fire within me

Relight the central candle, if you wish, or simply let the moonlight shine upon you, blessing you with the magic of Midwinter. Give the Lady an offering, and close the circle when you are ready.

Blue Moon

As the blue moon can happen at any point of the year, I will leave you to come up with a ritual that is suitable for your environment. Here are some suggestions for your blue moon ritual.

The blue moon is a time of heightened magical power, as well as a time for personal transformation. Though many people think that a blue moon is the second full moon in a calendar month, it is actually the third full moon out of four in a season (sometimes the two coincide).

Use this moon for an additional boost to spellwork in the ritual or to initiate a change in one's self. It's a great time to do a hedge riding as well, so try to incorporate that into this special time.

Black Moon

Similar to the blue moon, the black moon is the third dark moon in a season that contains four dark moons. This is a time of high psychic energy, so it is an incredible time for divination work of any kind. It's also a good time for consulting the ancestors and deep meditation. Go with what your heart tells you do for this black moon.

Exercises

- Do any of these moon rituals resonate with you? Some may, but some may not, as your local environment may greatly differ. Can you create your own set of lunar rituals that correspond to where you live? Give it a go.

- Take some time each day to study the phase of the moon. You should know the moon phase at all times in the back of your mind, so keeping a daily track will help you get into the rhythm.

- Try performing a ritual for different phases of the moon, not just the full moons. Try creating a dark moon ritual of your own or a first or third quarter moon ritual or a gibbous moon ritual. See how these different lunar energies flow in a ritual context.

Suggested Reading

Praise to the Moon: Magic & Myth of the Lunar Cycle by Elen Hawke (Llewellyn, 2002)

A great book written from a British witch's perspective on working with the moon tides and creating your own magical practice.

A Witch Alone: Thirteen Moons to Master Natural Magic by Marian Green (Thorsons, 1995)

A brilliant book all about how to work with the moon tides, this is an excellent work for both beginners and those who want to brush up on the foundational lore from a British witch's perspective.

I stand on the shingle spit, a long finger of stones that has been rolled smooth by the sea, reaching out toward the eastern horizon. I'm almost half a kilometre out in the sea with just this thin, raised piece of ever-shifting stones keeping me out of the water. It's a beautiful, liminal, in-between place that is neither sea nor land but something that is always changing, constantly flowing. It's always different each time I visit, and tonight at the full moon the low tide is really, really low, meaning that even more of this unique phenomenon of the shingle spit is visible. I walk where it is safe, for here if you misstep, if you think you're walking on sand, you're more likely to be sinking rather than walking. This is a strange, alien landscape, one that must be respected, one that is wild and free.

The waves are rolling in from all sides. There is a river mouth to my left and the open sea to my right. Here at the tip of this little strip of stones is where all the worlds seem to be coming together. I plant my staff with a garland tied to it, white ribbons flowing in the ever-present sea breeze. I look straight ahead to the east, and just then the tip of the moon rises from the horizon, glowing a deep pink colour. I stand and watch the moonrise, the waves flowing all around me, the sound of shingle rolling forwards and back, forwards and back, lulling me into a trance-like state.

When the moon is higher and turns to her silvery light, I take out my drum and begin to sing for her. The wind whips my hair in every direction, and the skies darken as the setting sun's last light fades in the velvety night. I am utterly alone yet surrounded by the spirits of air and water, earth and fire. The stars shine all around me, the wind frees my heart from the daily struggles, the

water soothes my soul, and the stones ground me. It is utterly exhilarating. I dance and drum and sing to my Lady with wild abandon.

My full moon ritual that night is something that I will never forget.

Chapter 14

Working with the Otherworld

Fairies, come take me out of this dull world,
For I would ride with you upon the wind,
Run on the top of the dishevelled tide,
And dance upon the mountains like a flame!

. . . .

William Butler Yeats,
The Land of Heart's Desire

This book would not be complete without a chapter that further discusses hedge riding and working with the otherworld, with more rituals for betwixt and between. If you are new to hedge riding, I will briefly discuss it here, but for more information, please see my previous work *The Path of the Hedge Witch*.

More Rituals for Betwixt and Between

Hedge riding is an ancient tradition associated with Witchcraft. In fact, there are iterations of this practice from all over the world, and hedge riding is simply one aspect of a very powerful magical act performed by those who dare, who are skilled, and who seek to bridge the gap between this world and the otherworld.

Hedge riding is a trance practice that uses symbolism related to the hedge in various forms. Hedges are liminal places—areas that define one place from another. When we straddle this boundary, we are able to walk between the worlds. The popular image of the witch riding her broom is, in fact, a form of hedge riding. Whether we are performing a hedge riding in the physical or the astral, we are still working and walking between the worlds.

There are many different techniques to hedge riding, and they all vary according to the practitioner. First, a trance state must be attained through whatever means works for the hedge witch. This could include chanting, drumming, rocking back and forth, treading the mill (an old Traditional Witchcraft method), or even imbibing herbal potions (I don't use herbs for this purpose, but other hedge witches might). After the trance state is reached, many hedge riders visualise the hedge. This visualisation again can take many forms, such as a low hedge one can run toward and then leap over into the otherworld or a hedge with a gate or hole in it through which one can walk. Some may even visualise themselves straddling their broom (a symbol of the hedge and the world tree) and flying on their brooms to the otherworld. All these methods are really a form of astral travel, sending part of the soul out to the otherworld to gain the information and help that you seek.

You can also perform a hedge riding in the physical. Going out to a wild, liminal place and entering into a light trance, the practitioner can then cross between the worlds by using a physical landmark as the boundary between this world and the otherworld. This might be a gap between two hawthorn trees, a real hedge, a gate or a stile, crossing a stream, or any other significant liminal physical phenomena that works for the hedge rider.

Once in the otherworld, whether in the astral or the physical, the hedge witch uses their guides and their knowledge of the realms beyond to find out what it is that they need. One can perform a hedge riding to talk to the ancestors, the Fair Folk, the gods, or even for spellcrafting ideas and tips. Often the familiar or the hedge rider's fylgja can accompany the hedge witch on their travels to help and protect the hedge rider while exploring the otherworld. When the information is obtained or the work is done in the otherworld, the hedge witch returns to this world through a pre-ferred chosen method whether in the physical or the astral. It is important to return fully so that you can continue in your work without suffering any ill effects from your magical journeys. Hedge witches often have a foot in both worlds or are at least open to the ideas and inspiration from both this world and the otherworld. However, we fully understand that it is in this world that we live and work and where we need to ground our magical activities. We do not forsake one world for the other. We are walkers between the worlds.

You must be mentally prepared before you take on this work. It really does help to know thyself, as in all magical workings. When we are strong in the knowledge of ourselves, we will be more confident and capable in our dealings and forays with the otherworld and its entities. We won't be fooled by glamours or lies in any world we operate in. We won't be swayed by our own ego and wish fulfilment either. We know what it is that we wish to achieve, and we go out and do it.

We have developed our ability for discernment, so we will be safe, or as safe as we can possibly be, in our practice. We know which methods work best for us, and we are still willing to try something new. We feel the pull of the otherworld and the knowledge and experience that is held within, and we answer that call as hedge witches. Riding the hedge is what makes us hedge witches and separates us from similar paths such as that of the Green Witch, the Hearth Witch, the Kitchen Witch, and so on.

There are many different ways to perform a hedge riding. I offered several in my previous book, such as hedge riding in the astral, hedge riding in the physical, and treading the mill, as well as the tools that can be used for this work. I offered a ritual to ride the hedge, find your fylgja, find your fairy companion/guide, meet the deities, and more. Here I will offer further rituals that you can either perform or use as inspiration in creating and further developing in your own hedge witch tradition. Some involve hedge riding and some do not, but all are pertinent to the hedge witch.

Please ensure that you have read the introductory work of my previous book before attempting the following rituals, for without the foundation and basics of hedge riding and Hedge Witchcraft, you might unintentionally cause harm to yourself or others.

Dark Moon Mirror Scrying

Here you will find instructions on how to make and use a dark mirror for scrying. When you are scrying in the mirror, you are seeing both this world and the otherworld as per your intention. This is a great tool for getting a glimpse of the otherworld without fully doing a hedge riding ritual, so when time is short, it can be used as a quicker way to access the information that you desire.

A quick note: though it is called a dark mirror, there is no silver-backed reflective surface in this item. The intention is to have a completely black surface as opposed to a regular mirror.

How to Make a Dark Moon Mirror

Find a photo frame that appeals to you and seems magical. The photo frame should still have its glass, but if not, you will need to get a piece of glass cut to fit the frame. Good places to look are in antique shops and secondhand or charity shops. The frame may be made of any material: wood, silver, pewter, ceramic, etc. Try to keep the colours dark or muted to suit the purpose of the mirror. You can even use a large, flat, dark crystal such as obsidian for your mirror. It should be at least palm sized for ease of use. It's best to create your scrying/dark mirror during the dark moon period and only use it at that time.

To make your dark mirror, paint one side of the glass with a black paint. This can take many coats and needs to be completely opaque. For an easier solution, simply cut out the photo frame shape from black cardstock to fill the photo part of the frame. Place it in the frame and then cover it with the glass.

Once you have your mirror, wash it well by mundane means: this may mean soap and water or a damp cloth or a baking soda polish (if your frame is made of silver): just make a thick paste with a bit of water and rub it onto the glass with your hands, and then wipe/rinse off and dry immediately with a towel. When the mirror has been cleansed by mundane means, it's time to magically cleanse it and ready it for the work ahead.

You can use a purifying incense to magically cleanse the mirror, passing it through the smoke three, seven, or nine times. If you can't use smoke, take the mirror outside on a windy night and allow the breeze to blow it clean.

Now you can consecrate the mirror for your work. Make an infusion of mugwort tea, and gently rub the glass on both sides with the tea. Dry and set aside.

Keep your mirror covered in a dark cloth or in a special bag when not in use. Do not allow the light of the sun to reach it. Your mirror should only be used for scrying work.

You can also create a special ritual to dedicate your mirror to a deity and connect their energies to it. I call upon a local goddess, Andraste, in the dark moon mirror work as per the ritual below, or you can simply call upon the energies of the dark moon itself.

Dark Moon Mirror Scrying Ritual

Here I present two different uses and rituals using a dark moon scrying mirror. You may find many other uses for it, and I urge you to explore and find out for yourself all the things that this useful tool can provide. A dark mirror is not something that is especially related to Hedge Witchcraft, but it is a tool that has been used in Witchcraft for many years. I have even seen a Victorian dark mirror on a television show that dealt with antiques! In my own work, I use a dark mirror at the dark of the moon because I feel that this is the best time for scrying work. You may find other times in the moon's cycle more beneficial, so go with what works for you in your own practice.

• • •

At the dark of the moon, I tend to work with a local Celtic goddess, Andraste, whose name means "she who has not fallen" or "the indestructible."[56] With her deep, dark energy, she can help guide me toward maintaining my personal sovereignty. For it is under a moonless sky when I turn inwards to look at the shadow aspects of myself to better understand

---

56 Green, *Celtic Goddesses*, 32.

myself and in doing so, better understand others. In this ritual, we use the mirror to show us our shadow and light selves, as well as how to work with them to create a balanced and sovereign whole.

For this ritual, you will need a scrying/dark mirror, a candle (real or battery powered), and an offering.

Find a place and a time where you will not be interrupted. Light the candle and place your offering to Andraste (or any other deity or being that you are working with) upon the altar. Place your dark mirror upon your altar or hold it in your hands so that you can look into it. Perform the Roots and Branches meditation[57] or any other meditation that you use to ground and centre yourself. Connect with Andraste (or your deity or being of choice) through your own prayer of words from the heart. Listen for a reply.

When you are ready, look into the mirror. Say the following or something similar:

Lady of the dark moon

Mistress of the night

Guide me in my quest

Strengthen my sight

Show me my shadow

Unfocus your eyes and simply allow any images that may appear. You may see these moving in the mirror as shadowy images or as static images or even symbols. Let them come. Sometimes the mirror will remain dark, and nothing will appear. Do not worry, this takes practice. After a few dark moons you will get there. When no more images appear, take a few breaths and centre yourself once again.

Think about the images that you have seen. Look deep inside your soul and see how these images may relate to your shadow self. Journal them; see if they correlate to past experiences that no longer serve you. See these outmoded patterns of behaviour and make a commitment to change.

---

57   van der Hoeven, *The Path of the Hedge Witch*, 155.

You may now wish to scry in the mirror again for images that pertain to your sovereignty. You may also simply scry to gain a glimpse of the future. Take your hand and wave it over the mirror three times to ready it for your next working. You may wish to say:

> Andraste, woman to woman, I call to you: aid me
> to see my sovereign self; guide me to victory.

Watch as images appear. Words may also come into your mind—memories of past times when you were in your sovereign state. Reach for these, grab hold of them, and take them inside you. Make them a part of your soul. These will become your guiding beacons toward your full potential.

• • •

Alternatively, you can simply use the mirror for "regular" scrying purposes at the dark of the moon. This is an excellent time for getting glimpses from the otherworld of what it is that we need to know. To perform this work, you may say these or similar words as you prepare to scry in your dark mirror:

> Mirror of darkness and of dreams
> Help me to see what needs to be seen
> Guide me to the knowledge I seek
> Through these words I now speak
> Reveal to me what I need to know
> That harmony in my life may flow

Sit and look into the mirror. Unfocus the eyes and let the images appear. These will often be shadowy or even silhouetted images. Keep watching until they no longer appear, and then, as soon as you can, write down everything that you have seen. This is essential, for even the smallest portion may escape your memory and yet be utterly significant.

Hedge Riding to Meet the Ancestors

In this ritual we will cross the hedge in order to meet with the ancestors. There are many different types of ancestors that we can try to meet on the other side, such as our own blood relatives, the people who have lived on the land before us, or even spiritual ancestors of your current path. This ritual can be used to meet ancestors that you have known or those whom you have never met. This is a good hedge riding ritual to perform around the time of Samhain, when the veil between the worlds of the living and the dead is especially thin. Either way, it is a good first step in establishing a relationship, and therefore a new way of accessing information and developing your Hedge Witchcraft practice.

For this ritual, you will need your hedge riding tools, if any, as well as an offering for later and food to eat directly afterwards for grounding purposes.

Perform your hedge riding as is your custom. Once you have crossed over, ask your fairy companion, fylgja, or familiar to help show you the way to the realm of the ancestors. This may or may not be within the usual realms of your previous hedge riding experiences. Remember, it is different for everyone, for there are many ways to access the realm of the ancestors.

When you have arrived at the entrance to the realm of the ancestors, say these or similar words:

> Ancestors, I call to thee (name the type of ancestor, i.e.,
> a blood relative, spiritual ancestors, etc.), come meet
> with me betwixt and between the worlds as may be.
> I bring offerings and respect and desire to meet thee
> through the riding of the hedge and the world tree.

Wait a few moments and see if anyone appears. If they do, question them respectfully to ensure that they are who they say they are. Don't forget to get affirmation of their character from your guide, familiar, or fylgja as well. When you are satisfied of their nature and character, then ask them what it is that you need to know, or simply have a chat and be friendly. These are people with whom you may be working with in the future, so it is well to establish a good relationship now. Keep the first meeting a bit brief if this is your first time in this realm; you don't want to overtax yourself at this point. When it is time to go, tell them that you have an offering for them on the other side, which you will give to them in thanks. Bid farewell to them and allow your guide, familiar, or fylgja to take you back to where you can ride the hedge to this world. Perform your hedge riding to come back, and give the offering to the ancestors with these or similar words:

> Ancestors, I thank you for your time, for aiding
> me in my spiritual quest. I honour you and the
> knowledge you share and bid you a peaceful rest.

Now it is time to eat; in doing so, you will fully ground yourself back in this world. Leave the offering for the ancestors out overnight, if in your home, or leave it in a special place outdoors. Afterwards, remove the offering and place it in the compost or dispose of it accordingly.

Hedge Riding for Healing

This hedge riding may be performed to help heal yourself or another person. Magical ethics apply, as well as all the responsibility and consequences.

When we require healing for ourselves and others, we often forget that healing is not just in the physical realm but also in the energetic and spiritual realms. Holistic healing practices acknowledge this, and when used, they help heal the body, mind, and soul. In this hedge riding, we will seek healing for the condition as well as confront the source, if applicable, and find ways to bring about what it is that we need to address, redress, or make whole again in our selves.

Perform your hedge riding as is your custom. Once you have crossed over the hedge, your guardian, familiar, or fylgja is there to meet you. Greet them and spend some time with them as you would normally do, and then ask them if they can help you with your healing. Tell them what you need healing for, and listen to what they have to say. You may need to seek out and find certain areas, people, and things in the otherworld that can help you in your healing journey. It may not be a "one and done" affair. This will be different for each person, so I cannot go into much detail here.

What I can suggest is that you listen to the call of your heart, the advice of your guides, and your desire for healing. They may take you deep into the otherworld to meet with ancestors who can open up the doors of ancestral healing. You may be taken into the past, where wounding and trauma must be addressed before the quest can continue. You may even meet up with your fetch, if you haven't done so already. As stated earlier in this work in the section on familiars, the fetch will help you deeply understand your own self and may bring disparate parts of your being back together. If the healing that you require consists partly of soul retrieval, then this is most likely the work that the fetch can help you accomplish. Soul loss is a term used in shamanic practices where part of the soul is lost due to a traumatic experience or difficult stage in life, resulting in dis-ease, loss of energy, a feeling of incompleteness in life, and so on. Retrieving these parts of the soul helps heal deep soul wounds and bring about holistic healing.

Once you have begun your quest for healing, you may have to perform a series of hedge ridings to fully discover everything that you need to know in order to heal fully. This may take weeks or even months to complete, so don't worry that you haven't done all the work in this initial hedge riding experience. If the healing that you require is minor, then you may achieve your goal straightaway, but if it is something much larger, don't fret. You will find the pathways of healing that you need in your practice, with your guides and your guardians at your side.

As well, it is good to remember that not everything can be healed, and we are all part of the greater cycles of life, death, and rebirth. We work within those cycles and aren't separate from them. Therefore, we are bound to them and must learn from them in order for our own wisdom to grow. The information you may need regarding this can also be found in your hedge riding experience.

When you return from your healing hedge riding(s), ensure that you follow up in this world with everything that you can do to physically make yourself better (or the person that you are working for), as well as following the spiritual advice that you have received. The more mundane tasks, such as eating well and exercising, must be adhered to in order for holistic healing to occur. Take good care of your physical and energetic bodies.

Hedge Witch Dedication

This hedge riding can be used to dedicate yourself to your work in your own Hedge Witchcraft tradition. Should you so wish, you can perform this yearly as a rededication, which helps strengthen the bonds you have with this world and the otherworld. Part of this ritual takes place in this world, and part of it takes place in the otherworld.

Before this ritual, think long and hard on the dedication oath that you will use in this ritual. Write it down and refine it, and memorise it so that you can work more freely. Know that what you are saying will reverberate across all worlds, so ensure that it is truly spoken from the heart.

. . .

Create your ritual space as desired. Take a few deep breaths, and when you are ready, state your dedication oath to your hedge witch practice out loud. Put your hands on the earth and push that intention out into the world. Once you have done this, then perform a hedge riding and do the same on the other side. Words that you may use or be inspired by are:

> I dedicate myself as a hedge witch here
> In this world with all I hold dear
> May my magic be strong and insight be clear
> May I walk in darkness and light without fear
> May I walk and work betwixt and between
> With knowledge of the seen and the unseen
> May I gain true knowledge from my dreams
> Knowing things are not always as they seem
> In my hedge witch's work I am sovereignty
> And as this is my will, so mote it be

After you have performed this ritual in both worlds, ensure that you leave an offering and then celebrate in some special way.

Creating a Thoughtform for Protecting the Home

In this ritual, you will create a thoughtform through the energy of the otherworld, bringing it into being in this world to combine with your own personal energy in order to protect your home. You are not summoning a spirit from the otherworld; rather, you are drawing some of the energy that runs through the otherworld (much as you can draw upon the energy of this world through the elements of earth, air, fire, and water) and asking that it aid you in your work. Remember that there should always be a time limit on this, should anything happen, in order for the energy of the thoughtform to return to its original source. See the previous chapter on familiars to refresh your memory, if needed.

Find something that can house your thoughtform. A large stone, statuary, or something that corresponds to what it is that you have in mind is ideal, but you can go small and discreet should the need arise. Take time to get to know the object that will house the energy of the thoughtform. Study it, run your hands over it, cleanse and ready it for use. Then perform the following ritual:

• • •

Cast a circle or create sacred space. Have the object that will house the energy of the thoughtform with you in the circle. Call upon any guides, deities, or elements that you regularly partner with to aid you in your work. When you are ready, perform your hedge riding and enter the otherworld. Seek out the place where you feel the energy is right for what you have in mind and for your own home's protection. You can always ask your familiar, fylgja, or faery companion to help you, should you wish. When you have reached that place, call upon the energies of the otherworld in that location to aid you in your work. You may say something like:

> Otherworld energies, come to me, I pray
> In tune with my intention, guard my homestay
> Fill me with your power and cross the hedge with me
> To protect my home on the other side and blessed be

Feel the energies entering your body. Allow them to fill you up, and then thank them. Return back through the hedge in your usual way, still holding those energies. When you are fully back into your space, take up the object that will house the energies and push it from your body into the object. Stream all the energy into the object until you feel it has completely left your body. Now it is time to create the thoughtform with the energised object.

Hold an image in your mind of the thoughtform that you would like to create. It might look like the object, so if it is a gargoyle or grotesque, you may want to create a thoughtform that looks like the statuary. Or it could be completely different, say a warrior or a dragon that resides in a large stone by your front door. Either way will work as long as the image you have in your mind is strong. Fill the image in your mind with your intention to ward and protect your home, and when it is full, see it walking out from your mind and into the object. See and feel it absorbing the energies of the otherworld that are in the object, bringing it fully to life. This is now an entity that will aid you in your work, which consists of a part of you (the intention) filled with the energies of the otherworld. Now you must consider how long this entity will last and reside here with you before the energies dissipate back into the otherworld from whence they came. It could be a year and day or for your lifetime. You may say these or similar words:

> You are now an entity to protect my home
> A guardian spirit of place
> Work your magic in tune with my intention
> And ward this sacred space
> I task you with this duty
> For as long as I shall live
> And upon my death your energy returns
> To the otherworld I freely give
> Unless I deem it otherwise
> I shall instruct you likewise
> By the power of the earth, moon, and sun
> For the good of all and with harm to none

Close down your ritual space and place the guardian where you feel is best: for example, by your front door or secreted away in the garden around it if you want more discretion. Ensure that it is something that will not be easily stolen, if you live in an area where that is a possibility. If that is an issue, you can even place it just inside your front door.

Now you must ensure that you take good care of your guardian thoughtform, even as it is working for you. Make offerings to it; feed it some of your own energy from time to time. Greet it as you return home and say farewell every time you leave. Make sure that you introduce others that live with you to your guardian so that they know who is allowed to enter and be safe. If you need to do so on the quiet, you can always show pictures of those involved to the guardian rather than introducing them in person.

If you move, you absolutely must tell the guardian and take the object that is housing the energy with you to your new home. Leaving it behind will create all sorts of energetic havoc for the new owners and is very irresponsible. Introduce the guardian thoughtform to the new location and ensure that it knows what to do and who is involved. If you can't take your guardian with you for whatever reason, then you must break down the thoughtform and return the energy to the otherworld in a similar fashion to its creation. Simply do the reverse: take back your energy of intention, then perform a hedge riding to bring back the energy to the otherworld, from where you originally gathered it. Offer thanks at the end of the ritual and respect the energies that are involved in this special task. You may create a new thoughtform as needed when the time is right.

I return from the otherworld and close up my hedge riding experience. Taking a moment to fully return to this world, I lie down on the cool grass in the growing darkness. The skies overhead are dimming, and stars are beginning to appear. I drink in the night air, filled with peace and intention as I have just rededicated myself to my hedge witch's path. I have spoken to my Lord and Lady and my helpers on the other side of the hedge. I know what it is that I need and what it is that I can give back in reciprocity. I have a greater awareness of my place in the world and of where and how I fit in with my own environment. I feel more deeply integrated, sure of myself and my own powers and the road that I am walking in my own life. I'm content and level-headed, alone but not lonely, and assured but not arrogant.

A flicker of movement flits across the skies as I look at the stars. Another joins in, and I watch the dance of the bats in the late evening's light as they bless my ritual with their presence. An owl hoots in the distance and a muntjac deer barks nearby. Like them, I am part of this environment, seeking to thrive and be happy.

And I am.

Chapter 15

Integrity and Integration

A witch ought never to be frightened in
the darkest forest, Granny Weatherwax
had once told her, because she should
be sure in her soul that the most
terrifying thing in the forest was her.

. . . .

Terry Pratchett, *Wintersmith*

There is an awful lot of talk out there in the world. In fact, it can be quite
the challenge to stop and find the stillness from all the words, words, words
out there, the information that is coming at us from all directions. However, some of the talk is important, and even more importantly, walking
that talk brings us to a true perception of our own self and instils a deep
sense of personal integrity.

Words are important. They can help or harm, hurt or heal. They can
instil inspiration, courage, and fortitude in others—or they can do the
complete opposite. In this chapter we will look at the importance of our
own words, first and foremost, before we take a look at walking our talk.
Although words are important, our deeds say the most about how we live
our lives and who we are as human beings.

Integrity

As a hedge witch, you are beholden to no one except yourself. You set the standards; you decide what it is that you will do or not do. You decide on your own set of ethics and the moral codes you will live by. With input and information gathered and gleaned from the natural world and your friends, familiars, and the otherworld, you choose the path and the direction that you will take in your magical and spiritual life. However, there are still interactions with the world around you, and how you deal with certain situations has great impact upon your Hedge Witchcraft.

In Witchcraft there is the concept of the Witch's Pyramid. This provides a good framework for any witch who seeks to become more self-aware.

The Witch's Pyramid

Most modern witches, whatever their path, will come across the Witch's Pyramid at some point in their studies. The Witch's Pyramid is encapsulated by the phrase "To know, to dare, to will, and to keep silent," and it is most often used in the context of spellcasting. However, this phrase goes beyond just spellcasting. It is a guide for how we can be better people in general. Here we will explore each principle in some detail.

To Know

Those who follow any Pagan path tend to have inquisitive minds. They are willing to accept that there is more than the usual agreed-upon reality and that magic and mystery are all around us. They are not satisfied with the answers given by mainstream religions and quest for themselves the route to the divine in the form of the Goddess and the God. They hunger for spiritual and practical knowledge and experience and are unafraid to seek out the magic for themselves.

As many witches see their craft as a Mystery Tradition, self-knowledge is where we start. When we understand ourselves, we begin to understand the world. It means taking a long, hard look at ourselves and our behaviours, figuring out why we do what we do and the intentions that lie behind our words and actions. When we do this with intensity and discrimination, we will begin to understand where we deviate from our true potential and in our work in service to the deities and the world at large. In order to express the beauty and will of the Goddess and God, to celebrate them and life itself or the beauty of our own craft, we need to see beyond the filters of our perception, the many layers and veils of half-truths and deception, avoidance, and denial that we create around ourselves. We have to truly know ourselves.

In Jungian terms, this is to meet with and acknowledge the shadow, that part of ourselves which we would much rather deny. In knowing our shadow tendencies, we can work more positively in the world with true intention, instead of simply living reactionary lives based upon shadow impulses and behaviour.

The path of knowledge is an active path, not a passive one. It involves the seeker, the one on quest. We cannot sit back and have knowledge fall into our laps: we must go out and find it. We must turn information and intelligence into wisdom, and this is only done through experience. Experience is an active force that complements intelligence in order to bring about wisdom. You have to do the research: you have to read and talk to others. You have to do the work. Others can't know things for you on your spiritual path. You may have guides and teachers, but they are there to show you the signposts for the path that you are walking and not do the walking for you.

It is also about learning the basics of your practice and tradition. In all forms of the craft, this means to study and practice all that you can, to really do your homework. Read all that you can, do the rituals, and learn the correspondences and how to work with energy. Just reading about the elements and how they can affect spellcraft isn't enough; you have to truly know the elements intimately in order for your work to be successful, whether in life, ritual, or in spellcraft. Otherwise, they're just words, ideas, and empty symbolism without the true power that lies behind the imagery and knowledge.

As well, if you want to know how to do something, do it; don't just think about it. That's where true knowledge lies. Do your magic and spellcraft after doing the work and research, and then you'll become a real adept. Remember, it's experience that turns intelligence into wisdom.

To know also means to take responsibility for yourself and your work. You are a part of an ecosystem, so it is up to you to make your work beneficial to the whole. You have to know your place in the wider web so that you can work to create the change you want to see in a holistic manner. This also comes back to "Know thyself," for when you do, you will know where you fit in to the grand scheme of things and then are better able to effect change.

So, the first step on the Witch's Pyramid is to know both yourself and your path. You have to do the work, both in ritual and study as well as in your own person. Knowing who you are, where you are going, and why you are doing it will give you greater power over your life and the ability to respond to situations clearly and without misconceptions, for that is true responsibility. As it is written above the Temple of the Oracle at Delphi, "Know thyself."

To Dare

The second level of the Witch's Pyramid is "to dare." No, this is not a double-dog dare; it's bringing action to your thought. We began with "to know," and now we put what we have learned into action. It is walking your talk.

Lots of things may change for you as you walk the hedge witch's path. You may start to see the world differently, as different things will be more important to you than perhaps before you began walking this path. You may want to take more action in protecting the local environment or working with it, or joining the parish council so that you can help decide where the new housing developments will be in your local patch. You may get outside more, venturing further and further into the wilds, becoming a part of the landscape itself. You may begin to work magic, build confidence, and learn lots of new skills. You will change internally as you confront your shadow aspects and work to be the best person that you can be. This perhaps requires the most courage of all.

People on the whole do not like change, least of all change within themselves. It may seem much easier to try to get other people to change, when in reality changing ourselves is the only thing that we truly have control over in our own lives. Forget wasting time trying to change others; the change that you want to see in the world starts within you.

You will have to be strong and walk your path with discipline. As a hedge witch, you must seek your own answers to questions and dare to ask them in the first place. Simply walking a solitary path is daring for many who are uncertain as to their own ability. Dare to walk your own path. Dare to be different. Dare to be you.

Being different is hard for those who would rather blend in with the crowd. But walking and working in the world as a hedge witch means that you will be different; there's no two ways about it. The world is magical, though most people don't see it. The Goddess and God are real, though most people can't feel them. The Fair Folk, the spirits of place, the ancestors: they are all a real part of your life that others choose not to acknowledge, and this is what makes you different. You know that there is spirit in the stone, in the tree, in the fox, and in the badger. You know that the God and Goddess are within as well as without. You work in the world with this knowledge deep in your soul, and it dares you to be different—to explore the world of nature and Witchcraft more fully so that you are a contributing member to your own destiny as well as your own environment.

You may lose contact with some friends or family members who do not approve. People at work might treat you differently if you tell them you are a witch. There is absolutely no need to go around telling everyone who and what you are, and if you choose to conceal your true leanings, then that is the right choice for you. Only you can know whether it is a good or bad idea to out yourself as witch. But if you do, you will most likely have to face some people's ignorance and misinformation at some point, and possibly their own shadow projections on top of that.

You will have to dare to make your dreams a reality. You will have to dare to manifest in your life that which you want to bring about. You will have to dare to be strong and face certain truths about yourself and the world. It is the challenge given to us by the Goddess and God, asking us to take action, to get up off our butts and put our thoughts and words into practice.

We will have to dare to live for ourselves while accepting all our responsibilities. We will have to change, as our words and actions have great meaning. We will have to dare to face the truth that we have previously lied, cheated, or done a host of other unsavoury things in our lives, and we have to dare not to repeat them ever again. A witch's word means so much, as we will see later on in this chapter, and when we lie or use our words without thought, we lessen our power. We have to dare to speak the truth and our own truth, to allow our soul's truth to be in the world for what it is, and to be proud of who we are.

We will have to let go of aspects of our lives that no longer serve us. We will have to admit that our practice changes as we change, and dare to allow that evolution to happen. For otherwise we will stagnate, and there will be no personal growth. We also have to dare ourselves to challenge what we think we know, to broaden our perspectives and bring fresh light into our thoughts and situations.

Most of all, we have to dare to seek the truth without letting ourselves get in the way.

To Will

What is will? Well, most importantly, your will is your determination. It is your willpower. Do you have the energy to persevere in your path, in your work? What happens when others put you down or you find yourself not knowing quite which way to turn? Your will helps you to get through these moments, perhaps even guided by the hands of the Goddess and God. As they are immanent, they are deeply connected to your will and your self if you open yourself up to them.

Do you have the staying power to keep at your craft? Can you focus your research, your practice, and your spellcraft well enough to achieve the results that you seek? Can you determine the difference between desire and will? You may want certain things in your life, but wanting alone won't manifest them. Do you have the willpower to change things if they aren't working and to accept change in your life if and when it becomes necessary?

Being a witch means making certain commitments in your life. These commitments are entirely self-directed if you are a hedge witch, but they are still there. A witch's word is also their power. You may have to do things when you don't feel like it or when you would rather be doing something else. Discipline is especially important for the hedge witch and any solitary practitioner.

Others may challenge you, your beliefs, and your practices. Do you have the will to stay true to who you are and what you believe? Are you able to contend with these folks in a respectful manner? Can you find the calm, still point within yourself to allow others to question your own tradition? Questions and judgements may be thrown at you at any time. It's up to you how you deal with them responsibly and ethically. Staying true to your will can help you overcome these challenges. Will is following through; intention is nothing without the follow-through.

To Keep Silent

Many say that this final maxim of the Witch's Pyramid was used in order to protect witches from outing each other during the witch trials and persecution of the Middle Ages. I'm not sure if it dates that far back, in all honesty. Today, being silent about your witchy ways might allow you to keep your job or live in peace in a certain type of community. Though the prejudice against witches is lessening, it's still there. It's often handy to be able to do your practice right under the noses of some people who would otherwise contend with you. Most people I meet who don't already know me have no idea what I am or what I do under the light of the full moon or during Yule. I don't dress or look "witchy" in the usual sense that the media likes to portray: in fact, once a television channel asked me to demonstrate a ritual for Hallowe'en, but when they found out that I don't bother with the big robes and ceremonial stuff, they went elsewhere! Just as well, really; I prefer my quiet little hedge witch life.

The village witch, cunning man, and wisewoman knew that the silence of observation helped them in their path. When you can watch others, see their behaviour, and learn more about them, you will be able to help them. Being silent means to be observant, to quiet your own self so that you can see what is really going on around you. If you are able to control your emotions and come from a place of stillness within, you will be able to make the right choice in any given situation. Keeping silent teaches us the power of just shutting up every now and then and truly listening. You can't really listen if you aren't quiet.

It also teaches us that words do have power. We need to use our words responsibly, especially in this age of social media and the abuse of people through the anonymity of the internet. A witch's word is said to hold power: lies and half-truths spoken from the witch undermine the witch's power (this applies to all people and not only witches, in my opinion). Words can heal or destroy. For example, when we lie, we split reality from what is true into a new reality that we have created for the person we are lying to for whatever reason. They believe in that reality, for which you are responsible. Lies fracture reality, leaving us with less integrity to hold it all together. We must learn not to lie—not to fracture this reality—because each time we do, we lessen the power of our own truth and our own soul's integrity.

We humans tend to lie to avoid certain issues or situations instead of meeting them head-on. Yet we are not authentic when we lie or when we avoid certain situations through lying. We must use our will to keep to our sense of self and our own sense of integrity because that is at the heart of Hedge Witchcraft. Integrity and integration are inseparable. We seek integration with the natural world, but how can we do so if we lack integrity?

For example, we lie to avoid discomfort or responsibility. Instead, we need to be real, to be here now, to be truthful to ourselves and others even if it's uncomfortable (while still being kind). Power is lost through fracturing reality and not being truthful. The importance of spoken words in Witchcraft and also in spellcraft relies on this power. You can't believe in yourself if you constantly lie. You know when you are lying: it just feels wrong, even the little white lies that leave a little twinge in the heart. If you don't believe in yourself, your magic and your life won't work.

A little side note on the use of our words: you must learn to speak the truth about yourself, especially when you are speaking about yourself to yourself. Words have power. How you talk to and about yourself is a spell, so putting yourself down all the time is a spell. Saying hurtful or nasty things about yourself is a spell. Don't create that reality. Instead, speak the truth and be kind, especially to yourself. If you find that you are putting yourself down, ask yourself: Would I say that sort of thing to someone else? Hopefully not. It's not okay to say nasty or demeaning things to others, and it's certainly not okay to say it about yourself. We are far too often harder on ourselves than we are on others. A little self-deprecating humour to keep the ego in check is fine, but telling yourself or others that you are useless is a big no.

Being silent also helps us see the bigger picture. When we step outside of our ego and its chattering, we begin to hear the stories of others and see the grander scheme of things. We all have egos, and we need to learn to work with them in order to not be ruled by them. When we are ruled by our egos, we aren't living intentionally; we are instead living reactionary lives.

Being silent is also helpful in teaching us to be alone. With so many gadgets to hand distracting us from ourselves, we've forgotten how to be alone, how to be bored, and, yes, even how to be lonely. It's only when you truly deal with loneliness that you can come to understand it and work to improve your situation. Then again, there are the more solitary folk who prefer to be alone and who find solace in this space for themselves to work, heal, dance, and pray. When we have cut ourselves off from all other distractions, we begin to realise that we are never truly alone. We have nature, the gods, and the ancestors all around us all the time.

Keeping silent also means that your actions will always speak louder than your words. Lead by example. Those who actually do the work are probably the least to brag about it.

Personal Responsibility and Accountability

Do you defer responsibility in your life? Why? Adults are (or should be) accountable for everything that they do. Unless you suffer from a medical or psychiatric condition, you are one hundred percent responsible for what you do. Yet we often fall into childhood traps of avoidance, deflection, and lies in order to save ourselves from the uncomfortable reality of owning our actions. It's time to learn how to be an adult while still experiencing the childlike wonder and enchantment of the world. Yes, you can do both. It's the hedge witch's way, not an either/or situation. We can live in both worlds at the same time. We can be responsible adults while still working in our craft.

Integration

Walking your talk is perhaps the most important thing about being a hedge witch. How you go about your everyday activities is a reflection of your craft. Sometimes it can seem like "real life" problems get in the way of your practice, so it is more important than ever to remember to integrate your witchy life with your so-called mundane life. You can be a witch and pay the bills. You can be a witch and be on the parish council. You can be a witch as you do your grocery shopping. Below are some examples of how to integrate your witchyness with the adulting things you have to do in life.

PAYING THE BILLS. Do you just set up that direct debit or write that cheque without thinking? Instead, you could use visualisation to ensure that you will always have the funds to pay these bills in the future. You could write a charm for just such a thing, draw a pentagram, a dollar sign (or whatever currency you use) over your screen or cheque while you speak or sing the charm over it. Draw in the power of the earth and imbue your action with the fertility and fecundity of earth's energies.

CLEANING THE HOUSE. You are still a hedge witch when you have to scrub the toilet—true fact. There are all sorts of things that you can do when you are doing regular housework, even scrubbing the toilet. If you want to get rid of crappy thoughts, feelings, or situations in your life, visualise them as you are scrubbing, and then flush them away! Having a clean home makes a real difference to how you feel overall. Keeping your house fairly tidy and clean will have an impact on your mental and physical health. You don't have to have your home spotless, but you want to have a clean and tidy place where you can work and live. If time is of the essence, then just focus on one room a day. Ten to fifteen minutes is all it takes. After you clean, cleanse your house the witchy way: remove any lingering negative energies that you feel are hanging around. Use smoke or moon water and a fan or broom to sweep those energies out the window. Then fill that space with the good, loving vibes that you desire.

TAKING CARE OF THE KIDS. Instil in your children the values that are important to you and your craft, such as responsibility, accountability, honour, respect, and wonder. Teach them of the cycles of life, death, and rebirth as you live through the seasons together. Teach them to honour the earth and live responsibly on this planet. Again, lead by example. Children watch their parents closely, so it is very important to be what you want to see in the world.

AT WORK. It's 4:58 p.m. and your boss has just come over and asked you to get a presentation ready for tomorrow. You are tired, hungry, and basically fed up. What the hell are you going to do? It's time to get your witch on. Grab a cup of coffee and imbue it with energy, vigour, and inspiration as you say a little charm over it. Go to the washroom and wash your hands, asking the goddess of the waters to help you flow through or around any obstacles. Look out a window, if possible, and see a part of nature that can remind you of resilience. Then go and do the thing. And then maybe tomorrow have a little chat with your boss, if you can, about having more of a heads up the next time so that you can do your very best with the extra time provided, as well as pick up the kids from daycare without having to pay extra time.

HEALTH AND EXERCISING. A healthy body helps keep your thoughts in good order. Your physical ability isn't the issue; what matters is that you are healthy. No matter what your situation in life is, are you as healthy as you can be? If not, how can you improve? Are you able to exercise but just need to create the time and space to do so? Then do it! If you aren't physically able to exercise for whatever reason (and raining isn't a good excuse), are you eating well? What are you putting into your body to fuel you through your day? Good, clean whole foods are essential to keeping your energy levels and your power in good stead. Eating junk food all day will not lend your body the energy that it needs to be healthy, productive, and powerful. Leave off the carbonated energy drinks: they are just chemical cocktails full of caffeine. Have a cup of coffee or tea instead if you must have the caffeine. Snack on things that are good for you instead of sugary treats wrapped in plastic. Take good care of your body and it will take good care of you. The power that you need to live your witchy life depends on it.

GARDENING. Did you know that there is a bacteria in soil that actually makes you feel better when you come into contact with it? *Mycobacterium vaccae* is a natural antidepressant that improves your mood and makes you feel good.[58] Getting some natural sunlight also keeps your vitamin D levels topped up (with proper natural sunscreen, of course; protect yourself). Remember I mentioned exercise in the paragraph above? Gardening is great exercise. If you don't have a garden, see if there is an allotment that you can work at or a community garden. Even having pots on a patio or balcony to keep herbs for cooking or flowers for their charm is a good thing. Get outside and go for a hike on the weekends, if you can, and put your hands in the soil. It's all good—and very witchy.

58 Gardening Know How, "Antidepressant Microbes In Soil."

COOKING. We've already talked about eating a healthy diet, but you can witch-up your cooking from being a chore to being a bit of magic. Stir the soup clockwise (or deosil) to bring in health and fortune to those who eat it. Stir your tea or coffee counterclockwise (or widdershins) to banish tiredness or anything else you wish to get rid of at that moment. Empower and charge the herbs that you are using for that spaghetti bolognaise before you throw them in the pot. Say a charm for happiness as you bake a nice cake for a friend's birthday. The possibilities are endless.

STUDYING. You might be in school or studying as a mature student on a distance-learning degree or honing up on your Witchcraft knowledge. It doesn't matter what you are studying or where, but you can certainly employ a little Witchcraft to help you along the way. Invoke a deity that is associated with knowledge, wisdom, and learning. Inhale some fresh rosemary as you study for a test, to retain the knowledge in your memory. Cast a spell for a successful exam result, for sure, but then do the work and study hard.

TRAVELING. You're a hedge witch on the go. So be one! Say a little charm of protection as you leave your home. Wear a talisman for safe travel that you created. Invoke deities associated with travel, especially safe travel. Thank them when you have arrived at your destination.

. . .

These are just a few examples to get you thinking about integrating your Hedge Witchcraft into your everyday life. You are a witch all the time, 24/7. Don't be afraid to act like it (even on the sly), and you will bring more magic into your life than you could ever have dreamed.

I rake up the beech mast, the scent of the autumn leaves all around me. I whisper to the old tree who has been on this plot of land longer than my house has been. This beautiful beech tree has seen things, has witnessed humans coming and going, has stood fast through bitter storms and coastal winds. It has sheltered many birds and provided food for wild animals including the badgers, hedgehogs, and deer that visit daily.

I gather up the opened husks and seeds and pile them up on the ground next to the compost bins. This way, the little ones will be able to eat it still, and I won't be pricking my feet on the thorny mast as I walk across the garden.

A little dunnock hops along the grass underneath the witch hazel. It looks at me, completely at ease and calm. I smile and talk to it, and it hops closer. I explain that I am about to mow the grass in this area, and it looks at me with sleepy eyes that start to close. I get the lawn mower down the garden, plug it in, and give thanks that we had the money to install solar panels ten years ago. I can now mow the lawn with solar energy. How wonderful is that? I warn the little dunnock again that I am about to make some noise, and it hops under the bush and settles back in for an afternoon nap.

I mow the area, always keeping an eye on the little brown bird to make sure that it is safe. It doesn't appear hurt, but I haven't seen it fly. I turn off the mower when I'm done and sit down for a brief moment, allowing my body to cool. My gaze is on the mower in front of me, silent and still, and suddenly the dunnock lands on it, looking at me happily. So its wings are fine. It's just happy and comfortable being around me. How absolutely lovely.

I whisper a little prayer for the bird—for it to have a long, happy, and healthy life. It hops off the mower and across the grass, picking up a large winged insect on the way. It's not hungry yet and so drops back off into snoozeland under the bush with the insect still in its mouth. I am so happy and amazed that this little wild bird is so content right here beside me, never minding the noise this human makes in the garden in order to take care of it. Ten minutes later, the bird wakes up and gulps down the insect. I get up and haul the mower back up the garden to the shed, and when I return the little bird is gone. "Thank you," I whisper to the hedge and beyond. This little moment of magic in the garden is a memory that I will cherish forever.

Conclusion

We are all apprentices in a craft where
no one ever becomes a master.

· · · · · ·

Ernest Hemingway

The craft of the hedge witch is a journey that never ends but rather opens up new horizons and worlds to explore as we gain experience and knowledge in our lives. We never stop learning. Each and every day is an opportunity to learn more about the world, ourselves, and the worlds beyond the hedge. The craft of the hedge witch is gathering that knowledge and making good use of it in everyday life. Listening to the wild birds and beasts, following the cycles of the seasons, keeping an ear to the ground in the community: these will all help the hedge witch work better in their craft.

Knowing that you are a part of an ecosystem that is in turn part of a larger ecosystem, and so on and so on, allows the hedge witch to find their place in the world and be a contributing, beneficial part of it all, whether that is in this world or the otherworld. In the craft, it's all learning, all the time.

I hope that this book has helped you deepen your practice and inspired you to continue on your journeys, wherever they may take you. May your hedge riding help you gain what it is that you seek, and may your magic aid you in all that you do. May the craft truly be a part of your life, for the good of all.

And don't forget Glinda's advice in *The Wizard of Oz*: "You've always had the power, my dear. You just had to learn it for yourself."

Blessings to you.

Joanna van der Hoeven
SAMHAIN 2023

Bibliography

Beyer, Rebecca. *Wild Witchcraft: Folk Herbalism, Garden Magic, and Foraging for Spells, Rituals and Remedies.* Simon Element, 2022.

Boyer, Corinne. *Under the Bramble Arch.* Troy Books, 2019.

Brigham Young University. "The Life and Legacy of the King James Bible." Accessed November 16, 2021. https://exhibits.lib.byu.edu /kingjamesbible/translating-kjb.html.

Bruton-Seal, Julie, and Matthew Seal. *Hedgerow Medicine: Harvest and Make Your Own Herbal Remedies.* Merlin Unwin Books, 2008.

Campbell, Joseph. *The Hero with a Thousand Faces.* New World Library, 2008.

Carver, Courtney. *Project 333: The Minimalist Fashion Challenge That Proves Less Really Is So Much More.* TarcherPerigee, 2020.

Clare Library Online. "Biddy Early: The Magical Lady of Clare." Accessed February 21, 2024. https://www.clarelibrary.ie/eolas /coclare/people/biddy.htm.

Crowley, Vivianne. *The Natural Magician.* Penguin Books, 2003.

———. *Wicca: The Old Religion in the New Millenium.* Thorsons, 1996.

Curott, Phyllis. *Witch Crafting: A Spiritual Guide to Making Magic.* Broadway Books, 2002.

Davies, Owen. *Cunning-Folk: Popular Magic in English History.* Hambledon and London, 2003.

Dugan, Ellen. *Natural Witchery: Intuitive, Personal & Practical Magick.* Llewellyn, 2019.

———. *Practical Prosperity Magick: Creating Success and Abundance.* Llewellyn, 2022.

Experience Life. "Walking Your Talk: The Path of Personal Integrity." Accessed October 23, 2023. https://experiencelife.lifetime.life /article/walking-your-talk-the-path-of-personal-integrity.

Forest, Danu. *The Magical Year: Seasonal Celebrations to Honour Nature's Ever-Turning Wheel.* Llewellyn, 2016.

Franklin, Anna. *The Hearth Witch's Compendium: Magical and Natural Living for Every Day.* Llewellyn, 2018.

Gardening Know How. "Antidepressant Microbes in Soil: How Dirt Makes You Happy." Accessed October 19, 2023. https://www.gardeningknowhow.com/garden-how-to/soil -fertilizers/antidepressant-microbes-soil.htm.

Green, Miranda. *Celtic Goddesses.* British Museum Press, 1995.

Grieve, Maud. C. F. Leyel, ed. *A Modern Herbal.* Cresset Press, 1992.

Hawke, Elen. *The Sacred Round.* Llewellyn, 2002.

History Ireland Magazine. "Feakle's Biddy Early: A Victim of 'Moral Panic'?" Accessed January 26, 2023. https://www.historyireland .com/feakles-biddy-early-a-victim-of-moral-panic/.

Hollis, James. *A Life of Meaning: Relocating Your Center of Spiritual Gravity.* Sounds True, 2023.

Hopman, Ellen Evert. *A Druid's Herbal.* Destiny Books, 1995.

Horne, Roger, J. *Folk Witchcraft: A Guide to Lore, Land & the Familiar Spirit for the Solitary Practitioner.* Moon Over the Mountain, 2021.

Howard, Michael. *East Anglian Witches and Wizards.* Three Hands Press, 2017.

Hutton, Ronald. *The Triumph of the Moon: A History of Modern Pagan Witchcraft.* Oxford University Press, 1999.

Jung, Carl. *The Collected Works of C. G. Jung.* Vol. 9, Part 1, *Archetypes and the Collective Unconscious.* Routledge and Kegan Paul, 1968.

Khait, I., U. Obolski, Y. Yovel, and L. Hadany. "Sound Perception in Plants." *Seminars in Cell & Developmental Biology* 92 (August 1, 2019):134–138. doi:10.1016/j.semcdb.2019.03.006.

Kúnkele, Ute, and Till R. Lohmeyer. *Herbs for Healthy Living: Recognition, Gathering, Use and Effect.* Parragon Books, 2007.

Legends of America. "Moll Pitcher—Famous Fortune Teller of Massachusetts." Accessed January 30, 2023. https://www.legendsofamerica.com/ma-mollpitcher.

Levack, Brian P. *The Witchcraft Sourcebook: Second Edition.* Routledge, 2015.

Maple, Eric. "The Witches of Canewdon." *Folklore* 71, no. 4. The Folklore Society, 1960.

McGarry, Gina. *Brighid's Healing: Ireland's Celtic Medicine Traditions.* Green Magic, 2005.

Mills, Ash William. *The Black Book of Isobel Gowdie.* Scottish Cunning Ways, 2021.

Mooney, Thorn. *The Witch's Path: Advancing Your Craft at Every Level.* Llewellyn, 2021.

———. "Winter Calls for Silence." *This Witch Magazine.* Winter 2019.

Museum of Witchcraft. "Betwixt and Between: Isobel Gowdie, the Witch of Auldearn." Accessed January 26, 2023. https://museumofwitchcraftandmagic.co.uk/exhibitions/betwixt -and-between-isobel-gowdie-the-witch-of-auldearn-2.

New Scotsman. "Why You've More Than a Ghost of a Chance of Seeing a Spook." Accessed February 21, 2024. https://www .scotsman.com/news/why-youve-more-than-a-ghost-of-a -chance-of-seeing-a-spook-2512341.

Norman, Mark. *Black Dog Folklore.* Troy Books, 2016.

Pearson, Nigel. *Practical Craft Working in Modern Traditional Witchcraft.* Capall Bann, 2007.

Pennick, Nigel. *Secret Societies of Rural England.* Destiny Books, 2019.

Planet Patrol. Accessed February 1, 2023. https://planetpatrol.co.

Pliny the Elder, Johann Emerich, and Lessing J. Rosenwald Collection. *Historia Naturalis.* https://www.loc.gov/item/48031835/.

Purkiss, Dianne. *Troublesome Things: A History of Fairies and Fairy Stories.* Penguin, 2000.

Rakusen, India. *Witch.* Season 1, episode 2, "Natural Magic." A Storyglass Production for BBC Radio 4, May 25, 2023. https://www.bbc.co.uk/sounds/play/p0fp3g92.

Random Scottish History. "Sketches of Superstitions." Accessed January 23, 2023. https://randomscottishhistory.com/2020/12/31 /sketches-of-superstitions-saturday-july-18-1840-pp-206-207.

Roth, Gabrielle. *Sweat Your Prayers.* Tarcham/Putnam, 1997.

Ryan, Meda. *Biddy Early: The Wise Woman of Clare.* Mercier Press, 1991.

Starhawk. *The Spiral Dance.* HarperCollins, 1999.

Starhawk and Hilary Valentine. *The Twelve White Swans*. HarperOne, 2001.

Taylor, Astrea. *Intuitive Witchcraft: How to Use Intuition to Elevate Your Craft*. Llewellyn, 2020.

Telyndru, Jhenah. *The Mythic Moons of Avalon*. Llewellyn, 2019.

Thurman, Tanya. *Persuasions of the Witch's Craft*. Harvard University Press, 1989.

Unibroue. "Maudite—About the Legend." Accessed February 28, 2023. https://youtu.be/CFt0ZhZGA0g.

Up Circle. Accessed February 1, 2023. https://upcirclebeauty.com.

Use Less. Accessed February 1, 2023. https://www.youtube.com /@UseLess_dk.

van der Hoeven, Joanna. *The Book of Hedge Druidry: A Complete Guide for the Solitary Seeker*. Llewellyn, 2019.

———. *The Path of the Hedge Witch: Simple Natural Magic and the Art of Hedge Riding*. Llewellyn, 2022.

Visit Essex. "Walking with Witches." Accessed February 19, 2024. https://www.visitessex.com/things-to-do/walking-with -witches-p1341751.

White, Nancy E. and Richard M. Leonard. *Introduction to Quantitative EEG and Neurofeedback*. Elsevier, 2009.

Wilby, Emma. *The Visions of Isobel Gowdie: Magic, Witchcraft and Dark Shamanism in Seventeenth-Century Scotland*. Sussex Academic Press, 2010.

Winsham, Willow. *Accused: British Witches Throughout History*. Pen and Sword, 2016.

Wong, James. *Grow Your Own Drugs*. Collins, 2010.

To Write to the Author

If you wish to contact the author or would like more information about this book, please write to the author in care of Llewellyn Worldwide and we will forward your request. Both the author and the publisher appreciate hearing from you and learning of your enjoyment of this book and how it has helped you. Llewellyn Worldwide cannot guarantee that every letter written to the author can be answered, but all will be forwarded. Please write to:

Joanna van der Hoeven
⅗ Llewellyn Worldwide
2143 Wooddale Drive
Woodbury, MN 55125-2989

Please enclose a self-addressed stamped envelope for reply or $1.00 to cover costs. If outside the USA, enclose an international postal reply coupon.

• • •

Many of Llewellyn's authors have websites with additional information and resources. For more information, please visit our website:

WWW.LLEWELLYN.COM